GURDJI

Seeker of the Truth

GURDJIEFF

Seeker of the Truth

by Kathleen Riordan Speeth

and

Ira Friedlander

Bibliography compiled
by Walter Driscoll

HARPER COLOPHON BOOKS

HARPER & ROW, PUBLISHERS

NEW YORK, CAMBRIDGE, HAGERSTOWN, PHILADELPHIA, SAN FRANCISCO

LONDON, MEXICO CITY, SÃO PAULO, SYDNEY

 For information address Harper & Row, Publishers, Inc., 10 East 53rd Street, New York, N.Y. 10022. Published simultaneously in Canada by Fitzhenry & Whiteside Limited, Toronto.

FIRST U.S. EDITION

Bibliography compiled by Walter Driscoll.

ISBN: 0–06–090693–6

LIBRARY OF CONGRESS CATALOG CARD NUMBER: 78–246–96

80 81 82 83 10 9 8 7 6 5 4 3 2 1

Contents

Introduction 13

Origins 25

The Call 35

Companions On The Way 37

The Search For Ancient Wisdom 49

The Inner Quest In Christianity 63

On The Path Of The Buddha 79

Toward The Secret Heart Of Islam 89

Appendix 118

Bibliography 121

The London *Times*, November 12, 1949

Mr. George Gurdjieff

A correspondent writes:
Mr. George Gurdjieff who recently died in Paris at the age of 77 leaves in nearly every country in the world friends and pupils to whom he was the incomparable teacher of a way of life. His death has seemed to many the premature curtailment of a life that was strenuous to the last days. He was born in the Caucasus in Alexandropol in 1872 and studied under the well-known Russian scholar and musician Father Borsh, Dean of the Cathedral at Kars. Until the age of 40 his life was spent in archaeological and anthropological research in Africa, Central Asia and the Far East. Having reached the conviction that his researches had led him to a valid conception of the meaning of human existence, and having discovered methods, some ancient, others new, for the development of the powers latent in the human *psyche*, he founded in 1910 in Moscow the Institute for the Harmonious Development of Man. After the Russian revolution this was moved to Paris, which had been the center of his activities ever since.

Writers, including Katherine Mansfield, A.R. Orage and P.D. Ouspensky, as well as many scientists and medical men, have been among the many students attracted by his conception of human destiny and impressed by his practical methods. These have hitherto been known only to the circle of his immediate pupils, but in the year before his death, he decided to publish his writings and to permit practical demonstrations to be given of his methods of work.

Everything Gurdjieff did seemed to originate from within. When he became angry, as he sometimes did, his anger had the appearance of being deliberate, and it was laid on one side as soon as it had served its purpose. The dark eyes would then regain their twinkle, the stern olive-colored face would relax and the conversation would be resumed at the point at which it had been suddenly broken off.

Kenneth Walker
Pauwels, p. 104

"For while I have received no impression that M. Gurdjieff is by any means as outstanding intellectually, emotionally or practically as his faithful disciples suppose him to be, I am convinced by my personal experience of him that he possesses another quality that may be more important than any of the foregoing. This quality he possesses to a degree not merely superior to that of any other man whom I have ever encountered, but to a degree greater than it would ever have occurred to me could exist, had I not met M. Gurdjieff. It is the quality, not of mind or of feeling or of successful accomplishment, but simply of *being*. I have never failed to experience this in his presence; one (or I) cannot "put one's finger upon it," but it is most certainly there. It has always prevented my (otherwise frequently demonstrated) ability to challenge him even upon those grounds to which he constantly lays himself open to the most obvious challenge. I cannot account to myself for this, in other ways inexplicable, respect in which I hold him, than by my admission of the remarkable degree of being with which I am always impressed when in personal contact with him."

C. Daly King
The Oragean Version

“

G: Thirty years ago, twelve of us spent many years in Central Asia, and we reconstructed the Doctrine by oral traditions, the study of ancient costumes, popular songs and even certain books. The Doctrine has always existed, but the tradition has often been interrupted. In antiquity some groups and castes knew it, but it was incomplete. The ancients put too much stress on metaphysics; their doctrine was too abstract.

DS: Why did you come to Europe?

G: Because I want to add the mystical spirit of the East to the scientific spirit of the West. The Oriental spirit is right, but only in its trends and general ideas. The Western Spirit is right in its methods and techniques. Western methods alone are effective in history. I want to create a type of sage who will unite the spirit of the East with Western techniques.

”

Gurdjieff in conversation
with Denis Seurat,
Fontainebleau, 1923.
In Pauwels, L. *Gurdjieff* N.Y. Weiser, 1972.

The famous prophet and magician Gurdjieff appeared in New York accompanied by Mr. Orage, who was acting for him as a kind of Saint Paul . . . I had the opportunity of observing Gurdjieff while he stood smoking not far from me in the vestibule . . . His general appearance made one think of a riding master, though there was something about his presence that affected one's nerves in a strange way. Especially did one feel this when his pupils came on to the stage, to perform like a hutchful of hypnotized rabbits under the gaze of a master conjuror.

Llewelyn Powys
The Verdict of Bridlegoose, 1927
In Seurat, op. cit. p. 138

You would be wrong to judge his conduct according to ordinary human standards. There seems a richness within Gurdjieff which allows him to do things that would be wrong for your own limited selves. In a way he reminds me of the god Shiva.

Pauwels, p. 59

Introduction

George Ivanovitch Gurdjieff (c. 1870-1949) was an extraordinary man who, by all accounts, produced an indelible impression on those who knew him and whose life, whether at the bottom line a success or failure in the attainment of his aims, was certainly of noble proportions. The task he undertook was heroic: to discover the truth about the nature and purpose of life on earth, and then to communicate what he understood in a way that would be of practical help to contemporary people.

As every translator will attest, the rendition of ideas from one cultural and linguistic context to another is an act of creation in itself. For Gurdjieff, the problem of conveying the benefits of his lifelong quest in the East to men and women in Europe and America whose experience, attitudes, beliefs and habits were radically different in perspective, must have seemed as intricate and complex as weaving one of the Persian carpets he knew so well. His search had taken him to the huts of shamans and the lamaseries of Tibetan Rinpoches, to the ruins of Babylon and Crete, to the libraries and mosques and monasteries of Asia, and to the great religious centers of

Echmiadzin, Jerusalem and Mecca. Alone or with companions he had hiked, rafted, ridden horseback, sailed on rivers and oceans, taken trains and camel caravans, crisscrossing an area of thousands of square miles to gather, by whatever means, everything that tasted of deep wisdom.

During his wanderings he came upon the trail of an ancient society of masters, the Sarmoun Brotherhood. Disappointed by the level of knowledge and development of his contemporaries, Gurdjieff began to trace this lineage in the hope of coming upon a real school. Apparently he found the descendants of the Sarmoun and they gave him some training. With this help he was at last able to assimilate the fragments of the truth he had gleaned elsewhere and to formulate what he understood.

The first part of his life's work was essentially completed by about 1910, when Gurdjieff was in his thirties. He had in his possession a body of wisdom that demanded a fresh formulation to be useful for the time, the place and the people. Gurdjieff began to teach, first in Tashkent, then in Russia and the Caucasus and eventually, fleeing from wars, revolutions and political disorders, in Europe and America. He collected around him what one observer called "the most profoundly active secret society in the modern world."

His approach was empirical, pragmatic and flexible. He made experiments, observing what his Western followers did with the practices he gave, and made modifications and corrections as necessary. He wrote voluminously and each chapter was read aloud while he watched individual reactions among the audience. Always valuing process and human effect above intellectual systematization, he slowly developed the teaching that was his legacy.

Gurdjieff was harmonious, a man among men. It was on his face, in his posture and his dealings with others. In Tashkent, Paris and New York, those who remember him today still recall his extraordinary eyes. He utilized all opportunities and wanted others to be trained to do the same in his Institute for the Harmonious Development of Man. He sought the secret of how to behave on this earth before one departs. He was taught that self-observation was important as a period of study in which to become acquainted with oneself and understand how one should be in this life. He taught others how to utilize the energy given to mankind in order to overcome a lukewarm existence. He understood that to be alive could mean to be alive forever.

The earth is a school for the furthering of that which is essential. A harmonious man may be free, but he is still a man. He is a man who can act in any situation in the way that is required for the understanding of conditions and how they can be converted for purposes beyond the satisfaction of ordinary, superficial wishes. Gurdjieff was deeply compassionate, yet he was not angelic. He was a man who behaved with understanding and could change his mood at any time, sit down, listen and talk, helping another out of confusion with accuracy. As the dervishes say, he had learned how to be in this world but not of it. He had the ability to kindle within others an inspirational fire; he could show a person what he or she was. In his presence people were awakened for a moment.

It was possible for Gurdjieff to be, but not always to be with other people. "Personally," he once said, "I should be very glad if I could talk to anyone of the subjects that interest me without having to put myself on a level with their understanding and intelligence." Esoteric knowledge is not to be casually given out; one has to know what to give and when. First the principles must be stated, then nourishment and correction follow. Gurdjieff understood that he must put himself through observation, participation and experimentation. He constantly placed himself in situations of great physical difficulty, silence and prayer. Although he drove himself relentlessly, he understood the gyroscopic spin in his life; a balance was necessary. Food that has simmered is better than boiled.

Gurdjieff's teaching, always responsive to the conditions of the moment, defies ossification into a formal description. What can be presented in a book can only be in relation to it as the bones of an animal are to its living, breathing presence. And yet the sun-bleached skeleton of a creature can yield at least some knowledge of it, and may in fact inspire those who study the fossil to make their own search for its living exemplars.

Here, then, is one view of the bones of Gurdjieff's teaching.

The Human Condition

Humanity exists on earth to serve a definite role in the cosmic scheme of things.

This role involves the tranformation of energies.

It is generally served unconsciously and without individual benefit. We are as if asleep to the nature and purpose of our lives.

Each human being is born essential and acquires attitudes, beliefs and habits reflecting family and culture. What is real in the individual is forgotten in identification with the personality.

The result of this hypnotic process is that the adult human being is like a sleepwalker, an automaton, a machine whose functioning is fragmented and inconsistent and has little or nothing to do with the deeply buried individuality stifled within.

This "machine" thinks, emotes, works, procreates, lives and dies without free will, without choice. He or she cannot love, cannot do. All is reaction.

This is slavery, imprisonment. And it is not even

necessary. The slave has no idea what he or she is losing.

Human possibilities are very great. There is a way out, a way toward freedom, toward self-realization. It is possible to find truth and liberation within, if it is a real aim. Know thyself, always and everywhere.

Although we live in a remote and relatively insignificant part of the universe, help exists. There are forces that can aid us, could we but hear their call.

Our heedlessness contributes to the terror of the situation, for without recovering what is real, death is the end. Our energies will be reclaimed and the rest will return to dust.

Higher aspects of a human being are already developed and functioning. It is the ordinary functions that must be regulated and quickened, must be harmonized. This work can be accomplished through impartial self study in ordinary life. Witnessing one's life deposits something fine within us from which what is substantial can develop. And in the light of awareness much of what is wrong cannot take place, for it can only happen in the dark.

Self observation can prove one's own nothingness, one's utter mechanical nature. This horrible recognition is a great beginning, for only then can the burning questions arise.

The human machine is balanced in all its details. All functions strive to remain in equilibrium. Under ordinary circumstances change is virtually impossible. But what one cannot do alone, several may do together. The guidance of one who knows more, *is* more, is needed, and the help of others whose aims are like one's own.

As in the case of the legendary phoenix, "one must be born, but in order to be born one must first die, and in order to die one must first awaken. The awakening can be gradual, and occur at first in brief moments. But the death must be all at once and forever." Then, from the ashes of a thousand attachments, arises a real individuality, I, oneself.

On Spiritual Paths

Gurdjieff stated that there have been five major religious traditions in the history of the world: Buddhist, Hindu, Islamic, Christian and Lamaist.

Every religion has an outer and inner aspect. The outer or esoteric dogma and ritual and theology tells what is to be done; the inner or esoteric practice shows how it is to be done.

Within religions there are four ways toward self realization. The way of the fakir stresses physical mastery and develops will; the way of the monk uses prayer and devotion to heal the heart and transubstantiate emotion; the way of the yogi deepens understanding for a lucid and clear mind. Then, hidden from view and involving physical body, heart and mind, there is the way of the sly man, the fourth of these ways, which works upon all three parts of the human being simultaneously.

Ceremonies have value if performed without alteration. Prayer by recapitulation may have results. Each aspirant will understand these things according to the level of being which is attained.

The Evolution of Humanity

Humanity neither progresses nor evolves by nature. *One* can evolve; humanity cannot, for evolution proceeds only consciously.

Yet humanity must evolve or perish.

The process of social evolution is the process of individual evolution, the formation of a conscious nucleus within humanity. Even 200 conscious individuals would change the whole of life on earth.

The individuals forming this inner circle of humanity, though they evolved by different ways, always agree and understand one another. Misunderstandings belong to the outer circle of sleeping people whose confusion of tongues and inevitable discord attest to their ignorance.

In order to help others one must first learn to help oneself. People's consuming interest in changing others is a sign of laziness in working on their own evolution.

Wars cannot be stopped by ordinary means; they are the result of cosmic forces acting upon organic life on earth. The energy made available by mass destruction of life is necessary for the cosmos in the absence of consciousness in humanity.

The Cosmic Context of Human Evolution

Everything in the universe is weighable and measurable, and all matter is vibrating.

Everything is permeated by material of all levels and densities of vibration.

The rate of vibration of any material is higher the less dense it is.

As above, so below. All laws of the universe can be found in any completed phenomenon. Thus a human being is a microcosmos within which is reflected the entire cosmos.

There are two great laws in the cosmos: the law of three and the law of seven. The law of three describes the necessity for three forces: active, passive and neutralizing, which must be present in order for any event to take place. The law of seven indicates the precise relationships among any series of events proceeding in even steps except for two vulnerable points designated in the musical octave as the mi-fa and si do intervals in the do-re-mi-fa-sol-la-si-do sequence.

These two laws are shown on one ninefold symbol, the enneagram, in which the inner triangle reflects the Law of Three, while the line connecting the points 1, 4, 2, 8, 5, 7 indicates the sevenfold series going into unity: $1 \div 7 = .142857$. All complete sequences may be displayed on the enneagram, and nothing can be fully understood which cannot be arranged in it.

All matter we know is living, and all matter is intelligent. Intelligence is determined according to what kind of creature a being can serve as food.

For example, human beings need three kinds of nourishment: food, air and impressions. The assimilation of each "food" can be shown on an enneagram. Ordinary food is completely metabolized naturally. But air, to be fully used, requires additional energy at its *mi-fa* interval, the energy of self remembering. This is the "first conscious shock." Impressions require a "second conscious shock" to be fully used.

Complete metabolism of all three foods nourishes what is real, subtle and spiritual in a person and provides the finest energies necessary for higher emotional and intellectual functions.

On the Teaching Situation

Between ordinary life and the way there is a stairway, and it cannot be ascended without a guide. One must learn from someone who knows, and must subordinate his or her will to this guide.

During the ascent the student may doubt everything, even his guide. At the last threshold these doubts will vanish and the guide will be less necessary.

No one can ascend in the fourth way without putting another where he was. Thus as the higher one ascends, the more dependence there is on those following.

A guide may sacrifice some attainments to help others reach a higher level. If they do, he gets back what was renounced.

The guide will effect change if what he or she teaches is from a true esoteric origin, regardless of whether he or she knows it.

The level of the guide always corresponds to the level of the student. Yet the student can never see the level of the teacher. In the fourth way the elder in the work is the teacher in any situation. The higher the teacher, the more difficult for the student.

As they place great value on their time, teachers act as guides for groups. The group must be constituted by the teacher, and without the teacher no group work is possible.

When the task is finished, the group disappears.

On Groups

A group is formed for a definite purpose.

The leader must be able to trust the members. The members must trust each other.

In the fourth way the elder is the teacher. There is no need for a teacher of exalted rank.

It is necessary to tell the truth to the teacher.

The teacher temporarily takes the place of the "I" in the student.

Each member in the group is given tasks according to chief feature. There are also general tasks for which the whole group is responsible, and in which a mistake by one is a mistake by all.

A group can achieve together what an individual alone can never attain.

On the Intellect

Before awakening, the intellect is merely formatory apparatus, the mindless deliverer of slogans and associations. Yet of the three centers, head, heart and gut, this could be the highest center of all.

The intellect is a storehouse of knowledge, but knowledge without being is useless or even harmful to development. Understanding, which is knowing in all three centers simultaneously, is necessary for inner evolution. Knowledge and being must develop together lest one become a weak yogi or a stupid saint.

The intellect is the chief place of lying, speaking about what one does not know. In effect, the psychology of man is the psychology of lying. As inner work proceeds one may become less interesting and more colorless, showing that lying is diminishing.

Questions must be aching. Intellectual fitting games have no place in the work.

On Emotions

The emotional life of one who has not yet awakened is entirely made up of negativities. Even positive emotions, such as what goes by the name of love, are in fact negative, since this love can turn into hate.

Emotional explosions can use up the energy needed for self study and conscious evolution.

Ordinary life is slavery to internal considering: living and acting constrained by the opinion of others. Internal considering must give way to external considering, in which the needs and wants of others are taken into account.

Considering and the other negative emotions are all based upon identification, becoming lost or absorbed in what seems to be the drama of one's life.

The personality is made up of many subpersonalities or "I"s, and these are protected from one another by buffer zones of unconsciousness. The buffers must be lifted gradually, for if one saw the truth and could do nothing to change it, madness could certainly follow.

Everyone always acts for the sake of good as he or she understands it. But cultural moralities have nothing to do with real right action, which can be understood only by the human conscience, as deeply buried within as the lost continent of Atlantis.

Work on oneself must be accompanied from the very beginning by the struggle against the expression of unpleasant emotions. This is preparation for the second conscious shock.

The connection with the truth can only be made through the emotional center. To understand more we must develop the emotions, for it is as if we have an emotional organ of perception whose capacity could be more sensitive and subtle than the intellect in ordinary people.

On Sex

Sex is the principal motive force for everything mechanical. It is also the chief possibility for liberation.

The new birth possible for a human being depends as much on sex energy as does the birth of any baby. That same energy can be used to create life within the body. This comes about when the body is saturated with fine energy which at one moment crystallizes. Alchemy calls this transubstantiation.

For this to happen, sexual abstinence is necessary for some but not for others. Some need a great deal of sexual activity in the beginning of transformation and then less as the process continues. Still others need little at first, and then go on to have full sexual lives once the process is started.

Abstinence is useful if it occurs in all centers, and if the celibate knows what to do with the energy thus made available. Without exact knowledge it is better not to change one's sexual habits in any way.

Sex center is on a level with higher emotional center. If it worked with its own energy all other centers would work with theirs and take their subordinate places.

A central human problem is the abuse of sexual energy, the use of sex energy by other centers or the use of other kinds of energy by the sex center. The misuse of sex energy is always identifiable by a particular vehemence and uselessness of the act.

On Death

As we are, without inner evolution, death is the end for us. But immortality or existence after death is a possibility.

Higher bodies formed through inner work must be evolved simultaneously and the connections between them established. These higher bodies must be active relative to the lower body.

People who have become less interesting through inner work have had a taste of truth and have begun to die before they die.

If there is nothing to withstand external influences there is nothing to withstand death.

The idea of reincarnation is near the truth, but only approximate. It is perhaps more useful to consider this the only chance we have.

The only hope for humanity is that each individual could uncover the conscience buried deep within by realizing that he will die and, indeed, so will everyone upon whom his eyes rest.

ORIGINS

Gurdjieff's parents both came from very old and remarkable cultures peculiar to Asia Minor. His mother was Armenian. The Armenians are among the oldest races in the world whose language, folklore, and musical traditions are still intact. His father, a bard who knew by heart whole epics, songs, and thousands of verses and stories, traced his ancestry to a Greek family who had fled Byzantium when Constantinople fell to the Turks. The family, whose great wealth was in its many herds of cattle, then traveled throughout Asia Minor in search of good pasturage. They went to Cappadocia, in the heart of Turkey, and to the shores of the Black Sea, and finally to Georgia. Around the middle of the nineteenth century, Gurdjieff's father moved with his mother and his wife to the town of Gumri, on the Armenian plains that stretch from the Black Sea to the Caspian.

Gumri was an agricultural and commercial town surrounded by excellent pasturelands. Its climate was one of extremes: bone-chilling winters, muddy springs, and summers that were dusty and hot. The town was on one of the most heavily-traveled routes between Europe and Asia, and on its streets one could hear a polyglot babble of Turkish, Greek, Armenian, Persian and Arabic, as well as numerous other languages and dialects. Nearly all of the world's greatest religious traditions had some representation here, and many cultural heritages existed side by side with little or no mingling.

The family settled in the Greek quarter, where the houses are in effect built underground with entrances in the roofs. (This method of construction offers protection against the harsh climate and probably goes back 8,000 years.) It was in one of these houses that George Ivanovitch Gurdjieff was born. His passport gives his birthday as December 28, 1877, but he said that he was born in 1869. As with most of the events of his early life, we have only his own account of his birth, and, as with those other events, its description has a mythic quality. He reports in *All and Everything* that he was brought into this world by a midwife sucking on a cocaine lozenge, to the sound of a neighbor's Edison phonograph penetrating a hole in the window caused by a crazy lame goat. (Since Edison built the first phonograph in 1877, one may conclude that Gurdjieff's report of his birth has some aim other than factual accuracy.)

Childhood

In the late 1870s, a terrible battle erupted between the Russians and the Turks for possession ofArmenia. The district of Kars, which contained Gumri, was given to the Russians by the Congress of Berlin in 1878, and Gumri became Alexandropol. Troops were stationed in the town, the streets were widened, and Russian signs began to appear over the shops.

> At this period Alexandropol was not a town, but a conglomeration of villages and a place of various cultures. The Armenian quarter reminded one of Egypt, with its flat-roofed houses sprouting grass. From the hill beyond the cemetery, with its coloured onion-shaped domes, one could see the snowy heights of Mount Ararat, where Noah's Ark came to rest. The centre of the town was Russian, with a typical Oriental market, draughty stalls, coppersmiths crouched on mats, soothsayers, storytellers and jugglers. Gurdjieff's parents' house was in the Greek quarter, and the ravines on the outskirts were inhabited by the wild Tartars. Many

> worlds met in the town, the dreamers', the actors', the speculators', the merchants', and the warriors'. Above the tents and roofs, rose the mountain where life began to flower again for the Just, after the wrath of the Deluge.
>
> Pauwels, p. 27

The war had caused various tribes and populations to migrate from areas that had previously been isolated for a very long time. Descendants of the ancient Assyrians—Yezidis and Aisors—came into the valleys of the Kars district from the south, Armenians arrived from the east, Greeks from the west, and Gypsies and Esthonians came down from the north.

Gurdjieff's father had been the richest owner of cattle in the district of Kars, but he lost his entire fortune when a cattle-plague struck the area. Gurdjieff, the eldest of three children, was then about seven.

This must have had a considerable impact on the family, accustomed as its members were to what Gurdjieff describes as a "large and grandly maintained household." Grander still, however, was the elder Gurdjieff's outward calm and detachment, which made a considerable impression on his young son. After trying and failing to run a lumber-yard, the father took his growing family—three more children had arrived—to the nearby fortress-town of Kars. Its new rulers, the Russians, were busy reconstructing it, and a better living seemed possible there. He opened a carpentry workshop and made wooden articles.

Gurdjieff's grandmother, who did not speak Armenian although that was the language of the household, died about this time. With her final words, she instilled in the boy a unique quality of independence and awareness: "In life never do as others do," she said. "Either do nothing—just go to school—or do something nobody else does." At her requiem service, he obliged by skipping around her grave and singing an irreverent ditty.

Gurdjieff was devoted to his mother, and cared for her until her death in the 1920s. As for his father—Gurdjieff considered him a "remarkable man." As a bard, or *ashokh*, the elder Gurdjieff, nicknamed "Adash," belonged to the tradition of Homer. He was a walking library, a repository of traditions that went back many thousands of years. His repertoire included songs, aphorisms, tales from the Arabian Nights, stories about ancient peoples, heroes, wars, miracles, natures, and God. He frequently entertained his family late into the night with these, and gave public recitations as well, traveling throughout the region in the company of his son. During his youth, Gurdjieff also went with his father to contests in which *ashokhs* from as far away as Persia and Turkestan would improvise and chant. One of the epics Adash knew was about the Sumerian hero Gilgamesh. Gurdjieff heard Adash chant songs from it so often that the boy knew them by heart. Years later, he read a magazine account of the discovery in the ruins of Babylon of some four-thousand-year-old tablets inscribed with verses from the Epic of Gilgamesh that were almost identical to those songs. Another legend that made a strong impact on the boy was one Adash told of "the Imastun," a brotherhood of wise men with telepathic abilities; after the disappearance of Atlantis and the Flood, the Imastun had scattered throughout the world.

Education

Adash enrolled his son in the local school, and he also took it upon himself to provide two other forms of training for the boy. The first was the inculcation in the child of a stoical outlook. The young Gurdjieff

Alexandropol, showing the typical houses with earthen roofs.

was made to handle snakes, and sometimes he would find a worm or a frog in his bed. Early every morning, he had to rise from bed and bathe in the cold water of an outdoor fountain. In this way, he learned to overcome timidity and squeamishness and to take a merciless attitude toward his wish for personal comforts.

Gurdjieff's father told him many stories of the lame carpenter Mustapha, who knew how to do everything and one day even made a flying armchair. "By this means and by other persistent procedures, my father fostered in me, along with the desire to be like this expert carpenter, the irresistible urge always to be making something new," Gurdjieff wrote. "All my childhood games, even the most ordinary ones, were enriched by my imagining that I was someone who did everything not as it is usually done, but in quite a special way." It was his father's gift that in Gurdjieff there were high ideals and poetic images. And the tenacity instilled in him in his youth helped him to endure the bitter hardships and difficult situations which he confronted throughout his whole life.

The second form of training was subtler. It had to do with teaching by indication rather than by direct instruction. In Sufism, the esoteric core of Islam, teaching is commonly done through stories, poems, or actions, because the Sufis say of their knowledge, "when it is stated, it disappears." An *ashokh* like Adash would surely have been exposed to the influences and teaching methods of Sufism. Sir Richard Burton, who translated the tales of the Arabian Nights, considered them a compendium of Sufic lore. Many epics and legends are metaphors for the search for something higher or more extraordinary than ordinary waking consciousness. Teaching through tales, through aphorisms, through oblique references, through hints and clues is called "scattering" by some, and it is thought to be especially useful when the message transmitted must penetrate resistances in the student's mind.

From the Arabian Nights, often called the Thousand and One Nights. The Sufis say to look for the One in the thousand and the thousand in the One.

Gurdjieff would be working in his father's carpentry shop, making pencil boxes or other small objects, when his tutor, Dean Borsh of the Kars Military Cathedral, would enter the workshop and begin bizarre dialogues with Adash. In one of these, later described by Gurdjieff, Borsh asked, "Where is God just now?"

"In Sari Kamish," Adash replied. (Sari Kamish was a forested region on the Russian-Turkish border.)

"What is God doing there?"

Gurdjieff's father replied that God was making double ladders there, and was fastening happiness on their tops so that individual people and whole nations could ascend and descend. Gurdjieff, writing later of this game of spontaneous questions and answers, called it *kastousilia*, a term he thought might come from an Assyrian legend. When Gurdjieff began to teach in the West, and to write, he continued to convey his knowledge in this same way, by indication, by indirection, even by contradiction.

Adash's perspective on life was simple: "The fundamental striving of every man should be to create for himself an inner freedom towards life and to prepare for himself a happy old age." When Gurdjieff last saw Adash, on a visit to Alexandropol with P. D. Ouspensky in 1916, the old man was still hale, "with an inevitable pipe in his mouth and wearing an astrakhan cap," Ouspensky later wrote in *In Search of the Miraculous*. "It was difficult to believe he was over eighty. He spoke very little Russian. But with G. he used to speak for hours on end and I always liked to watch how G. listened to him, occasionally laughing a little, but evidently never for a second losing the line of the conversation and the whole time sustaining the conversation with questions and comments. The old man evidently enjoyed these conversations and G. devoted to him all his spare time. . . . " (p. 342) Some years later, when the Turks attacked Alexandropol, Adash died from a wound he received defending his home.

Apart from Gurdjieff's unusual upbringing, he was exposed outside his home to a variety of other influences that must have contributed to his burning wish to search for truth. He had the opportunity to learn several languages. Turkish in particular was to serve him on his far flung travels.

No record can be found of a "Dean Borsh," the dean of the Kars Military Cathedral and "the highest spiritual authority for the whole of that region." According to *Meetings With Remarkable Men*, he began tutoring Gurdjieff, perhaps because he liked the boy's fine singing voice as it was displayed in the cathedral choir. With Borsh and other tutors, Gurdjieff studied geography, history, mathematics, anatomy, and physiology as well as the Russian language and Christian scriptures. Dean Borsh hoped that such a range of studies would prepare the boy to become both a physician and a priest, a person capable of treating and healing all aspects of an individual. Gurdjieff's own preference was for science and technology. Dean Borsh would change any project his student was working on as soon as it became familiar and likeable. This was a lesson in the development of a character which was prepared to surmount any difficulties presented by any kind of work.

Encounters With The Miraculous

Gurdjieff witnessed some supernatural events for which Borsh and his other teachers had no satisfactory explanations. In one case, he saw a table turning at an impromptu seance. None of the books in the Kars library could account for this occurrence, and none of his respected teachers would take it seriously. On another occasion, his aunt consulted a fortuneteller who accurately foretold a hunting accident in which Gurdjieff was wounded in the leg. Gurdjieff was later visited by this man, who proceeded to enter a trance by concentrating his gaze on his thumbnail. He described visions he saw there regarding Gurdjieff's future. Again these predictions were "uncannily accurate."

In 1888, Gurdjieff was sitting in a park in Alexandropol making a carving for a customer—he had built up a part-time business doing carpentry, carving, and odd jobs—when he noticed a commotion among children playing nearby. He saw a little boy, visibly distressed, who was unable to leave a circle that had been drawn around him on the ground. Gurdjieff, after learning that the boy was a Yezidi, erased part of the circle and the boy escaped.

Gurdjieff was astounded. Here was another seemingly mysterious event, inexplicable to him and apparently not in accord with natural laws. There was nothing to keep the boy from simply stepping over the line—or was there? Gurdjieff, thinking the explanation might lie in understanding the human mind, consulted a physician in Kars who explained

The fortress at Kars about 1882.

the phenomenon as "hysteria." This label struck Gurdjieff as inadequate, and many years later he verified for himself the inability of a Yezidi to leave a closed circle.

Evidence of Yezidi influence resurfaced later in his own teachings and writings. The Yezidi, commonly (and erroneously) called "devil-worshippers," are Kurds who are members of the Peacock Angel cult, whose center is in the gorge of Shaikh 'Adi, near Mosul in Iraq. The Yezidis may be descendents of the Assyrians; in any case, they are a dying race. Wherever these semi-nomads settle, they plant groves. They honor as their founder Adi ben Musafer, who lived in the eleventh century, A.D., and who is said to have been a student of no less than three of the greatest Sufi shaikhs, Suhrawardi, Al-Ghazali and Gilani of Baghdad. Adi ben Musafer founded the order of Adauiyya Sufis, of which the Yezidi are probably the last remnants. He was a Muslim, yet the beliefs and practices of the Yezidi are considered heretical to Islam. Like other Sufis, he taught that "only he who dies shall live. . . . He who perishes for the love of God becomes the glorious garment of God, and he who approaches God by making his life as nothing shall find his life returned to him by God." This is a recurring theme in the works of Gurdjieff as well. However, unlike Sufi sects, the Yezidis believe that Shaitan (Satan) was a fallen archangel who is in the process of being redeemed and that thoughts of evil keep his presence alive in the world; the Yezidi therefore allow no mention of Shaitan, and even cross his name out of the Koran. This has given them great trouble and infamy in the Muslim world and caused them generally to be thought of as devil-worshippers. They are known as the Peacock Angel Cult because, although they worship a single god, that god is remote from human affairs and so it is necessary to pray to angels who are in charge of mankind. There are seven such angels, and the Peacock Angel is the most powerful. In Yezidi enclaves as remote from Mosul as England, Yezidis dance to hypnotic music before images of the Peacock Angel. Gurdjieff may have taken some of the system of movements that he taught in the West from Yezidi ritual.

There were other events that puzzled and fascinated Gurdjieff in his youth. How was it that a church ceremony in which prayers were addressed to a miraculous ikon brought heavy rains to end a drought in Kars on a hot clear day? How was it that in the Tartar quarter a dead man was animated by an "evil spirit" and made to walk? Dean Borsh had taught the boy that body and mind are intimately related, and that priests must minister to the whole person, with medical competence complementing their understanding of the mind. Yet where among the books on anatomy, physiology and psychology were such events explained, and how could a full understanding of human life exist without incorporating them? Somewhere, at some time, someone must have had this knowledge, and Gurdjieff was seized with a burning desire to know precisely "the significance of life of all breathing creatures, and in the light of that knowledge, the significance of human life." Resolving to find out at all costs, he began to be filled with a spiritual wanderlust.

THE CALL

The legend of an inner circle of humanity—a network of evolved human beings who possess special knowledge and who watch over the destiny of the human race—is well known throughout the Middle East and Asia. As mentioned, Gurdjieff had heard from his father of such a society, the Imastun, that had existed before the Flood, perhaps from the time of Atlantis. As the crossroads of many cultures, the region where Gurdjieff grew up must have also yielded supportive information.

This legend exists in Buddhism in the form of a belief in Arhats and Bodhisattvas. In the Vajrayana traditions of Tibet, the equivalent is a belief in the reincarnation of certain lamas—the Rinpoches. J. G. Bennett writes of this phenomenon in *Gurdjieff: Making a New World*.

> The Sufi schools, particularly those who trace their origin to Bactria and Sogdiana, assert that there is a perpetual hierarchy, headed by the *Kutb-i-Zaman* or Axis of the Age, who receives direct revelations of the Divine Purpose and transmits them to mankind through the Abdal or Transformed Ones and their followers. The tradition of a perpetual hierarchy is held by Sufi communities as remote in

> other respects as the Bektashis and the Naqshbandis.
>
> Bennett, p. 25

Bennett goes on to suggest that the Naqshbandis are the heirs to a tradition associated with a school that flourished for nearly two thousand years in Balkh, in Central Asia, and whose members, known as the Khwajagan, or Masters of Wisdom, exerted a powerful influence on historical events. Bennett also refers to the Sarmoun or Sarman Society and states that "sarman" can be interpreted as the Pahlevi word for bee, "which has always been a symbol of those who collect the precious 'honey' of traditional wisdom and preserve it for future generations." There is also a collection of Armenian and Syrian legends known as "The Bees", which refers "to a mysterious power transmitted from the time of Zoroaster and made manifest in the time of Christ." Thus, the Sarmoun Society, whose center was thought to be hidden away in a nearly inaccessible region, might have operated as the curator of traditions and knowledge going back many thousands of years. Bennett concludes from his research that the Khwajagan and members of the Sarmoun were quite similar. Another speculation is that the Khwajagan were the outer manifestation, the husk, of the Sarmoun.

Gurdjieff wrote in *Meetings With Remarkable Men* that he had come across references to the Sarmoun in a book called "*Merkhavat*" and that it was supposed to be a "famous esoteric school which, according to tradition, was founded in Babylon as far back as 2500 B.C., and which was known to have existed somewhere in Mesopotamia up to the sixth or seventh century A.D.; but about its further existence one could not obtain anywhere the least information. This school was said to have possessed great knowledge, containing the key to many secret mysteries."

The Sarmoun (brotherhood of bees) Monastery was also thought by some to be a place where knowledge was accumulated and stored in a special receptacle and only released at a particular time which would benefit the world. This special receptacle is man. Written on the walls of the Sarmoun's study chamber was the phrase "Work produces a sweet essence," an idea to which Gurdjieff submitted his entire life and attempted to instill into the consciousness of his followers.

Convinced, then, that there had been schools or communities in which real knowledge existed, and that this inner circle of humanity might still exist, Gurdjieff made contact with many diverse secret societies and religious groups, gaining access to "the so-called holy-of-holies of nearly all hermetic organizations such as religious, philosophical, occult, political and mystic societies, congregations, parties, unions, etc. which were inaccessible to the ordinary man, and discussing and exchanging views with innumerable people who, in comparison with others, are real authorities."

Gurdjieff spent at least twenty years in his travels at a time when one could meet and even study with "special teachers" of knowledge and understanding who were still linked to their source of wisdom. Gurdjieff was convinced that under certain conditions man could reach the highest levels of consciousness and being. He sought knowledge and the people who possessed this knowledge.

COMPANIONS ON THE WAY

> For years they travelled over mountains and valleys, and a great part of their life flowed past on this journey. But how is it possible to relate all that happened to them? It would be necessary to go with them and see their

difficulties for oneself, and to follow the wanderings of this long road. Only then could one realize what the birds suffered. . . . So then, out of all those thousands of birds, only thirty reached the end of the journey. And even these were bewildered, weary and dejected, with neither feathers nor wings. But now they were at the door of this Majesty that cannot be described, whose essence is incomprehensible—that Being who is beyond human reason and knowledge. Then flashed the lightning of fulfillment. . . .

The Conference of the Birds
by Farid ud-Din Attar
(rendered into English
by C.S. Nott)

In the course of his attempts to make contact with an eternal and unchanging core of true wisdom, Gurdjieff either joined or gathered around himself a group of twelve or fifteen men and one woman, Vitvitskaia, who were committed to the quest for hidden knowledge. They called themselves the Seekers of the Truth. It may have been through his meetings with Professor Skridlov and Prince Lubovedsky that he made his connection with this group.

Gurdjieff described Vitvitskaia as "inimitable and fearless," always wearing men's clothes. She participated in all the perilous expeditions of the group into the depths of Asia, Africa and Australia. It was intelligent for a woman moving through such dangerous, almost forbidden, territories to disguise herself as a man. Isabelle Eberhardt, a contemporary of Vitvitskaia, found it helpful to dress as a man when she traveled the dangerous geography of Algeria seeking membership in a Sufi order. She was accepted into an order and subsequently traveled with identifying talismans and passwords through areas where no other European, man or woman, would have been allowed to wander.

"There were all kinds of specialists among us," Gurdjieff later told one of his pupils. "Everyone studied on the lines of his particular subject. Afterwards, when we foregathered, we put together everything we had found." Gurdjieff's main line of research was the transformation of energy in the human body and the use of music, art, posture and gesture to affect the level of consciousness. He had found evidence in certain ancient civilizations of objective methods by which a melody could be so designed that everyone who heard it, without exception, would experience the same emotional response. He also found buildings so constructed that consciousness was affected (this was true in both pyramids and Gothic cathedrals) and dances so designed that the inner state of the dancer was exactly altered. Gurdjieff also collected dances, for in them he hoped to find the key to the mysteries of the human body and mind.

There is a dervish story which tells of this kind of esoteric music. Once, in the East, there lived a traveling master musician who had invented a small stringed instrument. Every court wished the honor of hearing his music. The fact that his face was unfamiliar caused many lesser musicians and poor men to attempt to pass as this great talent in order to gain the favors of the sultan.

One day this great musician came to the sultan's court. He was poorly dressed, and so when he claimed that he was the famous musician, he was thought to be just another imposter. "Take your rightful seat in this court," said the sultan. The musician walked to the sultan and sat in the throne next to his. In a secret language the sultan told his vizier what he thought of this man. To his shock, the musician made a comment in the same language. "Would you like to hear my musicians?" asked the sultan. "Yes," answered the musician. The sultan's musicians began to tune their instruments and soon were playing. "What do you think of them?" asked the sultan. "I'm afraid they are not very good," came the reply. "Then perhaps you would like to play for us," the sultan said.

The musician took his small stringed instrument from its cloth and began to play. Within moments everyone in the court including the sultan was laughing uncontrollably. Then the musician played another tune and everyone began to weep. They could not stop crying. The musician changed the tune again and everyone fell asleep.

He placed the instrument back in its cloth sack and quietly left the sultan's court.

Some Adventures

Gurdjieff met Vitvitskaia again in Rome. He had run short of money, and again used his genius to increase his income. At this time one could make a small living shining shoes in Trastevere, close to the huge Michelangelo sculptures. Gurdjieff obtained an armchair, secreted a phonograph under the seat with lengths of rubber tubing extending to the customer's ears, and attached a tray holding a decanter of water, vermouth and a glass. People from the curious to the rich waited in line to sit in the chair, listen to music, read a magazine and enjoy a refreshment as Gurdjieff shined their shoes. On one such day he encounterred Vitvitskaia, and they spent much time together, which may have formed the basis of her joining The Seekers of Truth.

Gurdjieff summered in Suram, in the Caucasus, with his fellow seekers, Pogossian, Yelov and Karpenko four years after meeting Ekim Bey in Constantinople. The friends climbed the Suram Mountain pass, explored the environs of Borzhom and Mikhailov and tried to discover unspoiled peoples.

The Seekers of the Truth once met to explore the traces of very ancient civilizations said to have existed in Siberia, and they went from Orenburg through Sverdlovsk. As a group whose compelling interest was the gathering of human knowledge of reality, they were undoubtedly drawn to Siberia for its shamanistic tradition which extends back into the remotest antiquity. The shamans of Siberia may have been the original technicians of ecstasy. Through initiations involving ritual death and dismemberment they were trained to enter trance states in which they learned mysteries of life and afterlife, of flight through air and mastery of fire (the ability to generate heat in the human body), and of the secrets known only to animals and disembodied spirits. Shamanistic trance was used for prophecy, magical control of rain and weather, and healing the sick.

As one chosen as especially talented for the role of physician-priest, the Siberian shaman courted altered states of consciousness, and by so doing gathered experiential knowledge with which he "completed" or cured himself. Often these states were induced by hallucinogenic drugs, the most common being fly agaric or *Amanita muscaria*, a potentially deadly mushroom that has been identified as the "soma" of the ancient Aryans.

Later in his life Gurdjieff visited the famous caves in Lascaux, France, where a bird-headed shaman is depicted in a moment of ecstatic transformation near a bird-topped pole by which he is to make his ascent to attain immediate contact with celestial realities. The same ascent to heaven is reflected in the Indian rope trick in which a young disciple climbs a rope, disappears from view, and the *fakir* throws a knife into the air seemingly dismembering the youth. The rope is a ladder connecting heaven and earth.

When Moses came down from the mountain his skin radiated such light that the people could not look at him. When he finished speaking he covered his face with a veil. The light coming from him was so intense it looked as if he had horns, which may be why Michelangelo painted Moses with horns. The horns of light are the horns of understanding. Gurdjieff makes this reference in the chapter on "Impartial Mentation" in *All and Everything*. In the caves at Lascaux the animals painted on the walls had horns of varying lengths which, he said, represented the degree of understanding a person had attained.

The Universal Traveling Workshop

When visiting his family Gurdjieff would divide his time between Alexandropol and Baku, a town known for its bazaars. Besides his love for the open market, Gurdjieff was drawn to Baku to attend meetings of a mostly Persian society which studied ancient magic.

One day while "sniffing about the bazaar" Gurdjieff purchased an Edison phonograph from an old woman forced to sell her possessions. Out of pity Gurdjieff, who did not have much money, bought the seemingly useless machine. Upon arriving at the caravanserai where he was staying, he discovered that the machine had several recorded rolls and others which were blank. His money nearly gone, he thought of the possibility of making use of the Edison machine to earn money.

He traveled from Baku to the town of Krasnovodsk in the Transcaspian region. At this time the phonograph was still an unknown invention in those parts. He found a street musician who agreed to sing some local songs onto the blank rolls. Gurdjieff then attached two additional ear-tubes to the existing four and opened a booth at the bazaar where he charged five kopeks an ear-tube to listen to the music coming from this uncanny machine. Between the bazaar and private invitations, he made a large sum of money. He also accepted carpets in payment and accumulated a choice collection. In this manner he traveled from town to town until, on the train to Ashkhabad, he again met Vitvitskaia.

As a result of a wager with the fearless Vitvitskaia, Gurdjieff disembarked with the lady at Ashkhabad. There he opened a unique fix-it shop called "The Universal Traveling Workshop," or sometimes just the "American Traveling Workshop." The red letters on white cloth which hung in front of his rented store read:

American Traveling Workshop
Here for a very short time
Makes, alters and repairs everything

After distributing flyers announcing the occasion of the opening of this enterprise, Gurdjieff was inundated with every kind of gadget, machine, printing and manufacturing order, stamping, and more, and his ingenuity made him quite wealthy. At the time of this endeavor Gurdjieff was only 22 years old.

Like the "receptacle of honey" of the Sarmoun Brotherhood, the Universal Traveling Workshop, which could fix anything, solve any problem, and act accordingly in any given situation might represent man in the conscious state.

The Last Journeys

In 1898 The Seekers of Truth began a journey into the Gobi Desert in search of a city buried beneath the sand. So as not to follow the beaten track, they traveled with some difficulty from Tashkent up the Sharakshan River to F., a small place on the edge of

АБАКЪ
РАЗНЫХЪ ФАБРИКЪ
АПТЕКАРСКІЙ
МАГАЗИНЪ

The streets of Russianized Ashkhabad, where camel caravans and occupation troops coexisted at the turn of the century.

the desert. They mapped a route which would take them to the vicinity of this great buried treasure, where they planned to carry out some exploratory excavations under the guidance of Skridlov, the archeologist.

The Gobi was fierce. Legends described malicious spirits and demons who wandered the desert luring travelers from the protection of their companions. The wind often made strange noises which the mind transferred to invisible beings lurking behind sand dunes. This was the history of the desert handed down from the time of Marco Polo. Because of the difficulty in crossing the desert the group agreed that for the period of one month each would investigate certain problems and present a solution to the others. Some of the group's money was divided up and the members went their own ways, seeking solutions to the obstacles of the desert sands. A few settled in the village, and others left.

Throughout *All and Everything* Gurdjieff included all sorts of messages and teachings about common sense and the necessity of understanding and studying the drawbacks of any situation prior to becoming involved. Such common sense is explained in the chapter on "The Cause of Delay in Falling of the Ship Karnak." The captain of the spaceship tells Beelzebub of the impending danger of being hit by a great comet which leaves in its train a gas dangerous to the human body.

Beelzebub quotes from the Asian folk hero Mullah Nassr Eddin: "You cannot jump over your knees and it is absurd to try to kiss your own elbow." Beelzebub further explains, "There is nothing to be done; when an event is impending which arises from forces immeasurably greater than one's own, one must submit." Only after examining all the possibilities regarding the incident does Beelzebub decide to stop somewhere until the impending danger from the poison gas is past.

One month later the members of the group assembled in a small village at the edge of the Gobi Desert and, one at a time, discussed the solutions to the problems they faced. So incredible were these answers to what had at first seemed impossible difficulties that when each man finished his speech it almost seemed that this dangerous journey was "no more than crossing the Place de la Concorde in Paris."

Several days later, after applying certain physical practices and obtaining supplies, the itinerant band entered the desert. As they came close to where they calculated the buried city lay, Soloviev, "a passionate hunter and a dead shot," was killed by a wild camel which had bitten half through his neck. Using their rifles as a litter, they carried his body back to the camp whence he had wandered, and buried him in the heart of the desert. They all then agreed to leave the desert, and traveled west toward the Keriya Oasis.

Woven throughout Gurdjieff's life are stories which seem both plausible and allegorical. John G. Bennett felt that the Gobi Desert incident was told by Gurdjieff as a kind of "dervish teaching story."

> The role of Soloviev is from start to finish fantastical. The account of his death—with his neck gnawed by a wild camel in the Gobi Desert—upsets any possible chronology. He may probably be inserted here because Gurdjieff wanted to include the elaborate play-acting of the Gobi Desert adventure at this particular point. The entire group of Seekers of the Truth, including "the experienced astronomer Dashtamirov," who does not appear elsewhere, abandoned the undertaking "although they had already done much towards the discovery of

> the legendary city which they had expected to find on their journey." It seems to me that the whole story is an allegory of the search that looks for "real knowledge" somewhere "out there" as if it were hidden away in a legendary city in the midst of the Gobi Desert. In contrast with this, the Sarmoun sanctuary is "within" and it reveals its secrets to those who can die consciously as Prince Yuri did.

Where the Silk Road emerged from the Gobi the landscape changed and presented the traveler with Tibetan lamaseries and temples. This was a difficult area for Europeans to penetrate. But Gurdjieff and his Seekers of the Truth were not the only travelers who explored the hidden trails of Central Asia. In 1908 Sven Hedin, a Swedish explorer who was "drawn by the blank on a map," sought a different truth in the desert. To him, the parched wasteland was the ultimate challenge, something to be conquered at any cost. Regarding another explorer's decision to turn away from the dangers of the desert, Hedin once said, "In a similar situation I should never have made such a decision. I should have continued through the desert. It might have been the death of me and my men . . . but the adventure, the conquest of an unknown country, and the struggle against the impossible, have a fascination which draws me with irresistible force."

Hedin was mainly interested in opening unknown territory in geography, locating lost cities and physical features of the Asian heartland. Gurdjieff's was an inner search. Although drawn by the magnetism of certain areas, his aim was to gain new information that would enable mankind to succeed in the effort to transcend the lower self, the constant revolution which exists within us all.

By the turn of the century the Seekers of the Truth were preparing for a final expedition that would lead them through the Pamirs into India. They gathered at Chandyhou in the Transcaspian region and made their way through the narrow gorges and mountains of the Hindu Kush all the way to the northwest slopes of the Himalayas. The way was treacherous; Gurdjieff reported that two of the party died in an avalanche.

They met a dervish, probably a Naqshbandi, who healed ailments afflicting the travelers. He was able to show them how to get the right lumber for a safe raft and to give them accurate directions for sailing down a tributary of the Chitral River, which flowed into the Kabul River into inhabited country. This expedition came to an abortive conclusion for many of the band, however, as political unrest made travel in that part of the world increasingly hazardous. It was their last adventure together.

Along the way, in the course of numerous expeditions, several of the Seekers found—in various ways—what they sought. Gurdjieff was alone in his dissatisfaction and in his urge to seek further.

THE SEARCH FOR ANCIENT WISDOM

> "There are figures of gods and of various mythological beings that can be read like books, only not with the mind but with the emotions, provided they are sufficiently developed. In the course of our travels in Central Asia we found, in the desert at the foot of the Hindu Kush, a strange figure which we thought at first was some ancient god or devil. At first it produced upon us simply the impression of being a curiosity. But after a while

> we began to *feel* that this figure contained many things, a big, complete, and complex system of cosmology. And slowly, step by step, we began to decipher this system. It was in the body of the figure, in its legs, in its arms, in its head, in its eyes, in its ears; everywhere. In the whole statue there was nothing accidental, nothing without meaning. And gradually we understood the aim of the people who built this statue. We began to feel their thoughts, their feelings. Some of us thought that we saw their faces, heard their voices. At all events, we grasped the meaning of what they wanted to convey to us across thousands of years, and not only the meaning, but all the feelings and the emotions connected with it as well. That indeed was art!"
>
> —Gurdjieff as quoted by Ouspensky,
> *In Search of the Miraculous*, p. 27

At the time when Gurdjieff set out on his search, Minos, Nineveh, Babylon, Troy, Thebes, and other cities of the ancient world were becoming the objects of fervent attention from archeologists. Gurdjieff, having grown up hearing the same songs that had been sung in Sumer four thousand years earlier as well as legends of Atlantis and other myth-shrouded ancient lands, had a keen wish to explore these sites first hand. Perhaps clues to the fate of the Imastun Brotherhood of which his father spoke, or of the Sarmoun, might reveal themselves to him.

The Valley of Izrumin

Gurdjieff and his Armenian friend, a fellow seeker of truth named Sarkis Pogossian, decided to live near

Alexandropol among the ruins of the abandoned capital of ancient Armenia, Ani, "The City of One Thousand and One Churches." The Armenians have occupied the Anatolian Plateau since they crossed the Euphrates into Asia Minor eight hundred years before the birth of Christ and intermarried with the Chaldeans. Zoroastrianism was the predominant religion until the Christian era. Armenia is the oldest Christian state in the world, and the Armenian church is quite distinct in many ways from other forms of Christianity. Ani reached its zenith under the Bagratid kings, native rulers, in the ninth century after Christ.

Gurdjieff and Pogossian, digging among the ruins of the once-splendid city, found a crumbling monastic cell in which a stack of parchments had been hidden in a niche. The two young men went to experts for decipherment of these documents, which were in old Armenian, and learned that they were letters from a monk. They were written, evidently, about the seventh century A.D. and contained—to the great excitement of the two men—references to the recent migration of the Sarmoun Brotherhood from Mesopotamia to the "valley of Izrumin," near what is now the city of Mosul, and near Nineveh as well.

Gurdjieff concluded that the Sarmoun Brotherhood, which at some point had left Babylon for the Mesopotamian region, must have been comprised of Aisors.

The Aisors, widely scattered today, are all that remain of the race of ancient Assyrians. Some have adopted various forms of Christianity, and some have become Yezidis.

Gurdjieff had sworn that he would "ride the devil's back," if necessary, to find the Sarmoun. (Perhaps this is an oblique reference to the use he made of the Yezidi's so-called devil-worshipping cult to acquire secret knowledge. Bennett suggests that the valley of

Izrumin is actually the verdant gorge near Mosul that contains Shaikh 'Adi, the main sanctuary of the Yezidis.) Pogossian, who had also speculated previously on whether the Sarmoun actually existed, was equally determined. Episodes of violent political upheaval were commonplace in Armenia at that time, and travel was difficult. Pogossian managed to secure funds and jobs for himself and Gurdjieff as couriers for an Armenian political committee.

Disguised as Aisors, the pair traveled on foot through the wilds of Ararat and headed south toward their goal in Kurdistan. This region extends from the Zagros Mountains in Iran and the Taurus mountains in Turkey south across the Mesopotamian plain and includes the sources of the Tigris and Euphrates rivers. The men fulfilled only those assignments that brought them closer to their own real goal. Along the way they had various adventures, one of which inwardly terrified Gurdjieff at the time.

One day, they encountered several angry Kurdish sheep dogs. Pogossian threw a stone at them, which only caused them to become more vicious. Just as the dogs seemed about to attack, Gurdjieff pulled his friend to the ground. With this action the dogs were satisfied to simply bark and bare their teeth, and the men sat captive for three hours. A Kurd girl finally spotted them and ran for help, and soon the shepherds came and called off their dogs.

This incident is so similar to a dervish story that one wonders whether Gurdjieff included certain of these incidents in his life story, *Meetings With Remarkable Men*, precisely to teach:

A dervish studied with a shaikh for 30 years, then went to him and said that he would like to return to his village and teach what he had learned from the Koran and Hadis (the traditions, or sayings, of the Prophet Muhammad). The shaikh said, "I will ask you a question, and if you answer correctly I will know that you have understood what you have studied and I will give you permission to teach others. Where is your village?"

The dervish told him the name of the village.

"Are there any shepherds who tend their sheep where you will pass?"

"Yes."

"This question is not from the Koran, but if you answer correctly I will know that you have understood what you have read. What would you do if five of the shepherds' sheep dogs got angry and chased after you?"

"I would pick up stones and try to hit them."

"This would not be acceptable, because even if you hit one, at least four dogs would come from behind and attack you."

"Then I would take a stick and ward them off."

"No, my same answer still applies. Some of the dogs would get to you. I see you are still raw and not ready to teach."

The dervish begged the shaikh to reveal the correct answer.

"You should call loudly to the shepherd for help. He would come out of his tent and call all the dogs by name and they would not harm you. In the villages there are men who would treat you as these cruel dogs. If you try to fight them their attacks will be successful, but if you call out to Allah for help, He will stop them from harming you."

Once they crossed the Arax River, they were in Aisor territory and had to shed their diguises. They were very near Kurdistan when, in the course of a sojourn with an Armenian priest, they learned he had inherited an ancient document.

When he unrolled it I could not at first make out what it was, but when I looked at it more closely . . . My God! What I experienced at that moment! I shall never forget it. I was seized with violent trembling.

> . . . What I saw—was it not precisely what I had spent long months of sleepless nights thinking about!
>
> It was a map of what is called "pre-sand Egypt."
>
> Meetings with Remarkable Men

After obtaining a copy of the map, Gurdjieff and Pogossian immediately abandoned their aim of finding the valley of Izrumin, although they were probably only a few days journey from the site, and set off for Smyrna, where they boarded a ship bound for Egypt.

Egypt

> "Well then, my boy, Legominism is the name given to the successive transmission of information about long-past events which have occurred on the planet Earth from initiates to initiates of the first kind, that is from really meritorious beings, who have themselves received their information from similar meritorious beings. . . . This is the sole means by which information about certain events that proceeded in times long past has accurately reached the beings of remote later generations. As for the information which passed from generation to generation through the ordinary mass of beings . . . it has either completely disappeared, having been soon forgotten, or there remains of it, as our dear Mullah Nassr Eddin expresses it, only the 'tail-and-mane-and-food-for-Sheherazade.' "
>
> *All and Everything*, p. 351

Why did Gurdjieff so readily abandon his search for the remnants of the Sarmoun Brotherhood in Kurdistan? Did the map of "pre-sand Egypt" contain overwhelming evidence that he should redirect his search? He told Ouspensky, many years later, that the Christian form of worship was derived completely from Egypt, "only not from the Egypt we know but from one which we do not know. This Egypt was in the same place as the other but it existed much earlier. Only small bits of it survived in historical times, and these bits have been preserved in secret and so well that we do not even know where they have been preserved." (*In Search of the Miraculous,* p. 303.)

The Sahara, which now engulfs Egypt, developed only in historic times. Even during the Roman occupation, the desert was much smaller in area. In prehistoric times, the Sahara was covered with vegetation and dotted with large, shallow lakes.

If "pre-sand Egypt" has a symbolic meaning, perhaps it has to do with a special kind of consciousness, and the map might refer to a guide to oneself that has gotten covered up in everyday life.

Gurdjieff went to Alexandria, then made his way to Cairo and somehow, through his characteristic cleverness and industry, became a tour guide at the pyramids.

How were these massive monuments to death and the afterlife related to the quest upon which Gurdjieff had embarked? It was conjectured that the ancient Egyptians had precise knowledge of astronomy and mathematics and, furthermore, were masters of esoteric psychology. The famous Sphinx which Gurdjieff later spoke of as an example of conscious art was at that time buried up to the neck in sand. Only the questioning eyes and flattened nose confronted the desert visitor with their mute riddle. Yet this head alone produced an extraordinary effect upon the viewer, an effect that was undoubtedly specifically built into its dimensions, with the accuracy of deep understanding, by initiates of remote

In the foreground of the pyramids rests the Sphinx, as Gurdjieff saw it, buried to the neck in sand. It was not until 1850 that the Sphinx was first uncovered. It is covered by sand, every twenty years.

antiquity. According to Gurdjieff the Sphinx was emblematic of the bull, lion and eagle natures of mankind. The bull represented maleficent impulses in a person that can be transformed only by hard labors; the lion was to remind one that such labors should be performed with courage and faith in one's own might; the wings of the eagle suggest that while one performed such hard labors with self-respect, it was also necessary "to meditate continually on questions not related to the direct manifestations required for ordinary being-existence"; and the breasts "of the virgin" signified the impartial love that befits inner and outer work.

And the pyramids? In part, according to Gurdjieff, they were a portion of a complex of astrological observatories, some of which were underground, and in part they were designed to influence the surrounding climate! It may be that some of the meaning of the "pre-sand" map was clearer to him as he contemplated the pyramids and Sphinx. By chance a scholarly archeologist, Professor Skridlov, recognized the map. He befriended Gurdjieff and introduced him to his remarkable friend, Prince Yuri Lubovedsky, a lifelong seeker.

Prince Yuri was considerably older than Gurdjieff. He was also a man driven by the incessant wish to know the truth. They were both intrigued by Gurdjieff's map, and retired to the prince's apartment in Cairo to renew their conversation about the search. They became fast friends. Nourished by travels together in India, Tibet and various *tekkes* and monasteries in Central Asia, the two continued their loyal friendship by means of correspondence for 35 years. Finally he was taken in by initiates of an esoteric school on the condition that he die immediately and completely to his former life, give up all attachments to it, possessions and relationships, as finally as one dies to this earth, and the correspondence ceased.

Skridlov and Gurdjieff traveled on together, and lived for three weeks in a tomb in Thebes.

Babylon

Gurdjieff and Skridlov went to the newly excavated ruins of Babylon. Here German archeologists had recently made careful digs that opened the ancient city to inspection for the first time in millennia. Gurdjieff spent hours in contemplation among the ruins, receiving a very strong impression of the masters who had once lived, worked and taught there.

Gurdjieff was searching for real and certain knowledge about man and the universe. According to his account in *All and Everything*, he found important clues at Babylon about the basic laws under which we live, and in particular about the Law of Seven which describes the discontinuities that occur in all natural processes. These clues, he suspected, had been transmitted through time and space as far as Mont.-St.-Michel and to individual scientists such as Leonardo da Vinci.

Although most of the considerable wisdom of Babylon was lost forever, and the Sarmoun Brotherhood had evidently vanished, Gurdjieff nevertheless found evidence of sacred dances which had once been practical means of human development. These dances were also a kind of choreographic calligraphy in which precise teaching could be deciphered by those initiated into the code of gesture, posture and displacement. Each dance was like a book or a telegram, but one cast in a language few could read.

Later in his life, when he began to teach, Gurdjieff presented a large collection of such dances from many Eastern traditions and cultures. Was he following the thread of Babylonian objective art in gathering these dances? To one who understood their script, the dances in monasteries, *tekkes*, temples and even in the fields and farms of Central Asia could provide a

Ruins of Babylon and the foundation of the Tower of Babel.

clearly marked trail which might lead to the living remnants of the ancient wisdom at their root.

Crete

Throughout his search Gurdjieff used the political climate of the times to provide opportunities for the satisfaction of his deeper interests. His visit to Mount Athos was probably on the way to or from an early trip to Italy and Switzerland, where he may have been sent as a representative of Armenian nationalist groups to find support among like-minded people in Europe. The Turkish oppression of Armenians was becoming deadly serious. Armenians were massacred in Batum, outraged in their own homeland. They wanted and needed an international outcry on their behalf.

Gurdjieff could not have gone to Italy for the Armenians without stopping at San Lazzaro in Venice. This monastery, founded by the same Mekhitar from whose printing press came many books concerning Armenia, was second only to Echmiadzin as a center for Armenian monastic learning.

In 1896 Gurdjieff made his way to Crete, one year before the Graeco-Turkish War. There was political agitation in the area, and Gurdjieff probably made use of his Greek ancestry to make contacts and to join one of the nationalist organizations, a secret society called the *Ethniki Etairia*. The island of Crete is rich with clues to the ancient history of the Mediterranean area. Sir Arthur Evans had just discovered seals connecting Crete with cities in Mesopotamia. Could Gurdjieff learn anything in Crete about the legendary "flood before the flood" described in the Gilgamesh epic? Was the lost continent of Atlantis somehow involved in the transmission of the lineage of ancient masters of wisdom? His archeological researches were aborted by a bullet wound; unconscious, Gurdjieff was taken by some unknown Greeks to Jerusalem to recover.

Jerusalem

In Jerusalem Gurdjieff became a tour guide. This enabled him to earn a living and also to explore the holy places of the city. As he walked the Stations of the Cross he would have noticed the strange marks scratched into the paving stones. It was the game called King, played by the Roman soldiers as they awaited crucifixions. As a guide Gurdjieff would also have visited the Dome of the Rock, the Mosque of Omer, the Tomb of King David with its huge green sarcophagus, Bethlehem, and the Wailing Wall, all that remained of the Great Temple Of Solomon . On the street of Aqabat Dervish he might have paused to pray for the being in the tomb seen only by peering through the small window cut into the huge stone wall.

Not much is known about Gurdjieff's travels in and around Jerusalem. By means of a letter of introduction from Father Evlissi, a former tutor in Kars, he spent some time with the esoteric brotherhood known as the Essenes. This brotherhood, comprised mostly of Jews, was located outside Jerusalem near the Mount of Temptation. Members were under a vow not to marry, ensuring that the society remained secret and small (it is said that Jesus once lived with them). Only certain people were allowed to enter its ranks.

From these men Gurdjieff experienced certain "feelings" which later influenced his sacred dances. It was here that he learned of plants growing in half an hour by means of ancient music and songs. Later Gurdjieff would experience the influence of music in an incident with Vitvitskaia and would eventually describe it in *Meetings With Remarkable Men*. The chapter on the Bokharian Dervish in *All and Everything* contains his writings on the vibrations and influence of music on man and his psyche, and he explains in great detail this science in reference to

A painting of Jerusalem before the turn of the century.

the saintly Hadji Asvatz Troov, a dervish *shaikh* of great stature modeled after holy men Gurdjieff met during his travels. This old dervish experimented with sound vibrations with instruments he constructed and a pot of flowers which reacted differently when exposed to varying sounds.

THE INNER QUEST OF CHRISTIANITY

Gurdjieff often told his students that what he taught was simply "esoteric Christianity." Certainly he spent long stretches during his early travels in seeking out monastic centers where the earliest forms of Christian worship were preserved.

Cappadocia

Cappadocia, in the heart of Turkey, was a center for religion in the ancient world, and, as the result of a visit from St. Paul, was one of the first regions to convert to Christianity. On this high plateau, with its eerie moonscape topography of volcanic mounds, the Christian liturgy was created three or four hundred years after Christ. The great theologians who developed the liturgy wanted to connect the practices of the ancient religions with Christianity. "Every ceremony or rite has a value if it is performed without alteration," Gurdjieff once said. "A ceremony is a book in which a great deal is written. Anyone who understands can read it. One rite often contains more than a hundred books." He considered the liturgy just such a vessel of knowledge.

Perhaps that is what drew him to Cappadocia, where, he told friends later, he stayed for some time. Here there are monasteries cut out of the remains of the volcanic mounds. These were occupied by Greek priests at the time of his search. The sixteen centuries of Christian monastic tradition ended when the region's Greek population was expelled from Turkey in 1924.

Today the unusual landscape, the earthen pyramids, the monasteries, and the symbolic wall paintings in certain of the rock chapels still attract travelers who seek a truth hidden within an esoteric geography.

What everyone is in the eyes of God,
that he is, and no more. St. Francis of Assisi

Echmiadzin

Gurdjieff went to Echmiadzin, the hub of the Armenian religion, a place that had become the center of the church in 302 Common Era (C.E.), the year that St. Gregory the Illuminator converted the reigning monarch, Tiridates. But in Gurdjieff's youth Echmiadzin was a relatively small town on the banks of a stream that was almost entirely diverted to irri-

The earthen pyramids of Goreme in the heart of Anatolia in Turkey.

When you come to know yourselves then you will become known and you will realize that it is you who are the sons of the living Father. But if you will not know yourselves you dwell in poverty and it is you who are that poverty.

Gospel According to Thomas

gate the surrounding arid plain, then left to seep away into unhealthy, fever-producing marshes. Near it lay the ruins of Tiridates' capital city, whose 20,000 buildings attested to the antiquity of the place and its former cultural richness. There was still a bell with the Buddhist inscription OM OM HRIM, and upon the crumbling walls one could still make out tantalizing cuneiform inscriptions.

But practically no one—that is, nobody without Gurdjieff's consuming interest in hidden religious knowledge—would have bothered to explore the rubble of the ancient city. People came to Echmiadzin as pilgrims, to see the great Cathedral of St. Gregory and the minor churches around it. They also came to receive the blessing of the ruling patriarch, the Katholikos. Some came as seminarians to be trained in the Armenian tradition. The cloister was surrounded by a high mud wall upon whose heavy gates one had to knock hard and long to gain admittance. From the outside one might have thought it a Persian fortress. However, upon entering the gate it was clear that one was in a Christian monastery. Young trees sheltered the first court, the Pilgrims' Court, and it was there that visitors were accommodated. There were also trees around a charming lake within the garden, but outside the wall the plain was barren.

The glory of Echmiadzin was towering Mount Ararat, which rose in snowcapped majesty above the plain and which could not, it was said, be climbed all the way to the summit. Noah's Ark was said to have come to rest there, and a splinter from it was on view among the relics venerated in the cathedral. All Armenians know of the legend of a man named Jacob, a contemporary of St. Gregory, who wanted to put an end to the disputes about whether the ark had actually rested on Ararat. He wanted to see for himself, and resolved to scale the peak. As he climbed, however, he kept falling asleep. Upon awakening, he

Mount Ararat, where it is claimed Noah's Ark landed.

would find that he had slipped down the mountainside just as far as he had been able to ascend. Try as he might, he could not reach the summit.

At length, so the legend said, God took pity upon him and sent an angel to him in his sleep to tell him that the summit was unattainable, but as a reward for his efforts, and to satisfy the curiosity of mankind, he could have a piece of Noah's vessel. This very piece is preserved as a relic. The story of its acquisiton converted the popular belief that Ararat was impossible to climb into an article of faith to which Armenians affectionately clung. Other relics included the withered hand of St. Gregory himself, encased in silver, which was used ritually to consecrate every patriarch

The cathedral monastery in Echmiadzin, the spiritual capital of the Armenian church.

of the church. In Gurdjieff's time the hand was placed on the head of a most remarkable man, the beloved and charismatic Mekertich Khrimean.

The late nineteenth century was a time of political change within the church. The Russian government had begun to erode the ecclesiastical prerogatives of the clergy, requiring the Czar's approval of any newly elected patriarch. Russian policies excluded Armenians from civil positions, and Turkish oppression was an ominous reality in many cities, though Echmiadzin was spared.

Mekertich Khrimean was a man well known in the Armenian community for his published writings, and he had founded *The Eagle of Vaspurakan*, a journal widely read in his native province of Van. The proceeds of the journal allowed him to buy a printing press, then a great rarity in that part of the world. As abbot of the monastery of Varag he had used this press to print tracts reminding Armenians of their long history and dignity as a people. His writings were full of poetry and emotion as well as spiritual inspiration.

Khrimean was also widely known as a man of great personal presence. It was rumored that he had once been confronted by a would-be assassin, with rifle cocked and ready on his shoulder to shoot point blank. Yet this potential murderer had fallen to his knees, trembling before the unarmed Khrimean, unable to bear his glance. Such a man Gurdjieff would certainly have liked to question. And he was quite accessible. A contemporary British traveler gave this account of a visit with him.

> I do not remember having ever seen a more handsome and engaging face; and I experienced a thrill of pleasure at the mere fact of sitting beside him and seeing his smile, which was evidently habitual to those features, play around the limpid brown eyes. The

voice, too, was one of great sweetness, and the manner a quiet dignity with strength behind. The footman and dais and antechamber were soon forgotten in his presence—forms necessary to little men and perhaps useful to their superiors, though they are always kicking them off when they are not stumbling among their folds. Happily the temperament of his Holiness is averse to all baubles; the cross of diamonds is absent from the canonical cowl; and his black silk robe, upon which fell a beard which was not yet white, was unrelieved by the star of the Russian order. These ornaments are strangely out of place on such a figure, and their formulas out of keeping with this character. I was closely questioned upon all the incidents of our climb on Ararat; nor was it doubted that we had reached the summit. In the old days such a pretension would have been met with a smile. Then we passed to his sojourn in England, and I asked his opinion of Mr. Gladstone, with whom he had enjoyed some intercourse. He had been impressed, like so many others, with the theological cast of that supple mind. The face contracted when we came to speak of his life in the Turkish provinces; and he laid stress upon the terrible reality of the sufferings of the Armenian inhabitants. All the struggles and hopes and anguish of his strenuous days and sleepless nights seemed to rise in the mind and choke the voice. Then he sank back, with a sigh that seemed to regret them. "I have come," he said, "to the land of Forgetfulness." And from the quadrangle came the sound of a slowly-moving Russian anthem, and the measured steps of a detachment of Russian soldiers.

H.F.B. Lynch, *Armenia: Travels and Studies*. London: Longmans, Green and Co., 1901, p. 247.

A few days after this interview Khrimean, then 74, was ordained Katholikos in a solemn ceremony in the Cathedral of St. Gregory. It was October, 1896, and Echmiadzin was thronged with pilgrims who came to see their *hayrik* (dear father) crowned, and to receive his blessing. No one who could possibly have found a way to get there would have missed the great event. Was Gurdjieff present?

Sarkis Pogossian's search led him to study at the Theological Seminary of Echmiadzin. Although their families both lived in Kars and knew one another, the two young men first met in Echmiadzin. The two stayed together in Pogossian's small flat, and walked the streets of the town conversing on the nature of man and wondering aloud whether such an esoteric school as the Sarmoun Brotherhood really existed. At times they would also speak with some monks from the seminary, yet despite all the sharing of information, Gurdjieff finally left Echmiadzin, disillusioned at not finding any answers there.

Coptic Egypt and Abyssinia

For as long as the soul keeps running about everywhere copulating with whomever she meets and defiling herself, she exists suffering her just deserts. But when she perceives the straits she is in and weeps before the Father and repents then the Father will have mercy on her and he will make her womb turn from the external domain and will turn it again inward, so that the soul will regain her proper character. For it is not so with a woman. For the womb of the body is inside the body like the other internal organs, but the womb of the soul is around the outside like the male genitalia, which are external.

The Exegesis of the Soul
Nag Hammadi Library

With Professor Skridlov, Gurdjieff trekked southward from Cairo toward the source of the Nile. He formed the opinion that Egyptian Christianity was the expression of an ancient Egyptian esoteric school that had been carried on relatively intact with very little contamination. The Islamic rulers of Egypt had maintained a fairly benevolent attitude toward their Christian minorities, for after all, they too were "People of the Book" to whom revelation had been vouchsafed. Christians had been forbidden to intermarry with Muslims or to own property, but were allowed to practice their religion undisturbed. Little theological intermixture took place. Thus there was an unbroken oral and written tradition among Egyptian Christians, and much to study.

Coptic is the Egyptian language written with Greek characters. The Coptic Church is one of the very earliest Christian forms, and its desert fathers were very probably the progenitors of all Christian monasticism. Many of the early hermitages toward the mouth of the Nile were in almost total ruin at the turn of the century. But around the bend in the river just south of Thebes there were still monastic communities in which monks lived together in groups practicing the same ancient crafts, such as weaving, cobbling, and baking, praying together and preparing in a characteristically Egyptian way for their deaths. The rule they followed was that of Pachomius; their monastic life was cenobitic in form. It was group work, physical labor, in which practicalities of this world were performed within a context of otherworldly concerns.

It was near the earliest monastery of Pachomius that two ragged Muslim peasants discovered a jar containing priceless Coptic manuscripts almost half a century after Gurdjieff explored the area. These documents are called the Nag Hammadi Library after the place they were unearthed, and they rival the Dead Sea Scrolls in their historical significance. They also provide clues to what Gurdjieff may have found in the oral teachings and ceremonies of the Coptic monasteries he visited. What was found in that jar at Nag Hammadi gives us a taste of the gnosticism upon which Coptic Christianity rests, and which is strikingly different from more exoteric Christian beliefs. In a tract on the origin of the world, for example, God is portrayed as having erred in the Creation, and the tempter helped humanity by providing self-knowledge. In *The Exegesis of the Soul* the human spirit is likened to a prostitute who goes with any man as if he were her master— a harsh but moving allegory for the process Gurdjieff later called identification and against which his major practice, "self remembering," was directed.

Undoubtedly some of the real knowledge of the Coptic tradition was still present in the network of monasteries that lay along the banks of the Nile for 450 miles southward into Abyssinia. For three months the travelers explored the region. Then they made their way back toward the Red Sea, and during this part of the journey most probably went to the ancient but still functioning monastery of St. Anthony of the Desert. The monastery had an excellent library which even then was renowned in the Christian world, and it contained manuscripts which had not yet been purchased or spirited away by British collectors and treasure hunters. As at Mount Athos, it was necessary to have a letter of introduction to enter the fortress-monastery, but once received the traveler was given a hospitable welcome by the monks.

Mount Athos

You are aware that our breathing by which we live is an inhaling and exhaling of air. The organs that serve for this purpose are the lungs which surround the heart. They pass air through themselves and flood the heart with it. Thus breathing is the natural way to the heart. And so, collect your mind and conduct it by way of your breathing by which air passes to the heart and together with the inhaled air force it to descend into the heart and stay there. And train it not to come out of there quickly; for at first this inner enclosure and restraint is very wearisome, but when it becomes accustomed to it, then on the contrary it does not like whirling without, because it is there filled with joy within us, for now it sees it within itself . . . And you should also know that when the mind is established within the heart, it must not remain there silent and idle, but must unceasingly make the prayer, Lord Jesus Christ, Son of God, have mercy upon me! This prayer, by holding the mind without dreaming, renders it inaccessible and immune to the appeals of the enemy and daily leads it more and more into love and longing for God.

St. Nicephoros of Mount Athos
in Ignatius Brianchaninov,
On the Prayer of Jesus.
London, Watkins, 1952.

Gurdjieff visited Mount Athos around 1895. For almost a thousand years monastic life had existed there, unprofaned by the temptations of the world. Twenty monasteries, surrounded by their fields and farms, made up the spiritual community that filled the breathtakingly beautiful rocky peninsula in northern Greece. Each monastic group was autonomous, each different and unique. In the

Monastery of Sphigmenou 1871, at Mount Athos.

Monastery of Iveron 1871, at Mount Athos.

idiorhythmic orders monks performed physical work and spiritual practice individually, while in others, the cenobitic orders, there was less personal autonomy and more communal sharing. Some had even made provision for complete solitude, to the extent of lowering recluses into hermitages that were no more than caves in the seacliff. These hermits were provided with baskets of food by the parent monastery until the day, years later, when the provisions remained untouched and there was nothing more to do except remove the corpse by a rope so that another aspirant could withdraw forever in the same place.

This was a society of intensely spiritual men, a religious fortress. No woman, not even a female animal of any kind, had ever entered. Here Gurdjieff came searching for real wisdom, for more light on the questions that consumed his heart and gave his mind no rest. He probably arrived by sea, for the overland route was difficult and the excellent harbor just two days' sail from Constantinople.

No one visited Mount Athos casually; it was necessary to bring a letter of introduction from a high church official. Perhaps, given his close connection with the Russian Orthodox Church, Gurdjieff had entree to the Russian monastery of St. Pantaleimon, which lies on the southern coast of the peninsula quite near to the more famous monastery of Simopetra. The 2,000 monks of St. Pantaleimon followed an arduous schedule; they prayed standing up for eight hours a day and two more every night, never getting a full night's sleep. The rest of their time was spent working in the fields, mills and craft shops of their self-sustaining community. Every waking moment, day and night, these monks repeated the Jesus prayer silently and unceasingly: "Lord Jesus Christ, Son of God, have mercy on me, a sinner." The prayer was coordinated with the breath and heartbeat. It was rooted in a tradition that went back to the very beginnings of Christian monasticism, to the desert fathers in Egypt. The inner repetition also strongly resembled the Sufi *dhikr* and the continuous reiterations of Hindu and Buddhist mantras. In his teachings, Gurdjieff formulated the prayer as: "Holy Affirming, Holy Denying, Holy Reconciling, transubstantiate in me."

In 1892 one Brother Simeon left the Russian military service to devote his life to God on Mount Athos. When he entered his novitiate at St. Panteleimon he was given the Jesus prayer. Here is his account of his early experience of it.

> Brother Simeon spent a short while, some three weeks in all, praying the Jesus prayer, and then one evening, as he stood before he ikon of the Mother of God, the prayer entered into his heart, to continue there, day and night, of its own accord.

Brother Simeon went on to experience the profound visions and deep transformations that characterize the lives of adept in all the world's sacred traditions. Yet here were the undeniable signs of real inner change appearing within the Christian heritage of Gurdjieff's fathers. Could he have been looking for this? He undoubtedly met many holy men on Mount Athos, and perhaps even Brother Simeon himself. It is highly likely that, being of an experimental nature, he himself practiced the Jesus prayer.

The prayer of the heart was the core of a very well developed ladder of spiritual practices known to the fathers of Mount Athos and transmitted by them to aspiring monks. A rosary was used at first to count the prayers and the deep prostrations that accompanied them. But as the prayer absorbed the heart, the rosary became superfluous. The prayer was best said in a darkened cell to eliminate exterior distractions, and the eyes were closed. The left hand was placed gently on the skin above the left nipple. Often the monk sat on a low stool reminiscent of the dunghill from which the blind beggar of the Bible had cried out, "Lord Jesus, Son of David, have mercy on me!"

Like all potent spiritual exercises the prayer of the heart was considered too dangerous to practice without the guidance of a spiritual director, as the warmth it produced in the heart might excite sexuality or worse, produce the delusion of specialness that would erode humility. The prayer of the heart produced altered states of consciousness, and in a manner almost identical to that of the Japanese Zen masters, the fathers of Mount Athos warned their students to approach the prayer of the heart with prudence and caution, and to treat all apparitions that might appear with the utmost incredulity, considering themselves too fine to traffic with demons and too lowly to converse with angels.

Throughout his life Gurdjieff insisted that what he was teaching was "esoteric Christianity." He never broke his connection with the church, and even today memorial services for him are held, not among the straight-backed chairs of his silent disciples, but amid the candlelight, incense, chanting and mysteries of the Greek Orthodox Church.

Jesus said, "I took my place in the midst of the world, and I appeared to them in flesh. I found them all intoxicated; I found none of them thirsty. And My soul became afflicted for the sons of men, because they are blind in their hearts and do not have sight; for empty they came into the world and empty they seek to leave the world. But for the moment they are intoxicated. When they shake off their wine, then they will 'repent.' "

Gospel According to Thomas

ON THE PATH OF THE BUDDHA

Some highly educated Orientals with whom I have discussed Gurdjieff go so far as to maintain that he was simply a Buddhist who for personal reasons settled in the West and tried to teach us some of the simplest of the methods and truths known in the Far East.

Denis Seurat in Pauwels,
p. 121.

Tibet

While members of the Seekers of the Truth were busy gathering fragments of ancient wisdom, Central Asia was fast becoming a maelstrom of international intrigue and power politics. The British controlled India, Nepal, Sikkim, Bhutan and Burma, and were eyeing Afghanistan, Chitral, Kashmir and Tibet. China, traditionally interested in annexing Tibet, negotiated a treaty with the British that supported Chinese authority over that country. With neighbors to the south and east suddenly allied against his country, the Dalai Lama turned to Russia for help, sending the famous Lama Dorjieff as his emissary to Czar Nicholas II. But although the Czar was sympathetic, the complexities of the alliance took time. The mountains were high, the distance great and the matter delicate. It was a moment of great tension between Britain, China and Russia.

Gurdjieff later wrote that he had a "propensity during this period for placing myself wherever there were revolutions, civil wars, social unrest, both to understand this sole aim of mine in a more concentrated form and to somehow discover some way for destroying the predilection which causes them to fall so easily under the influence of mass hypnosis." It may have been his interest in human suggestibility that motivated him to continue eastward toward Tibet from the direction of the Karakoram at a time when international tensions made the Indian border virtually impassable.

Gurdjieff left practically no description of this expedition. Others who traveled in the same area at that time have, however, given us an accurate picture of the conditions that could be expected.

In 1901 the Swedish explorer Sven Hedin approached from Kashgar with his face blackened with soot to resemble a Buriat tribesman in an all-out effort to penetrate Tibet all the way to the Holy City. Even with the patronage of King Oscar of Sweden and the protection of the Czar he could get no farther than about one day's march from Lhasa. Surrounded by fierce Tibetan troops, he was forcibly detained until, by the express order of the Dalai Lama himself, he was commanded to retrace his steps. *Pelings* (Europeans) were forbidden to enter the Holy City, and an efficient network of spies made evasion exceedingly difficult. Sven Hedin's disguise failed, and although his royal patronage may have saved his life it was not enough to make him welcome, even at a time when the Dalai Lama's safety and the destiny of Tibet itself seemed to depend upon the kindness of the Czar.

With his swarthy complexion and Central Asian heritage, Gurdjieff may have fared better, though he probably also went in disguise. He may have made use of the similarity of his name to that of the Lama Dorjieff to enter Tibet and gain access to centers of learning which might otherwise have been closed to him. Even if he was working as a spy in the service of the Czar (as he might have been), if Sven Hedin's experience was at all typical this patronage would not have been particularly helpful as an entree to official Tibet.

The terrain in northeastern Tibet was quite arduous. The weather was unpredictable and violent.

A bridge swaying over a stream in Central Asia. Perhaps it was a span such as this that Gurdjieff crossed on his way to the Sarmoun Monastery.

Bandits and brigands, under cover of night or during the frequent downpours, would steal the pack animals, provisions and firearms of any foreigner. Why then would Gurdjieff have undertaken such a journey?

The Seekers of the Truth were deeply interested in making contact with an awakened inner circle of humanity, and the Tibetan tradition had an enduring and unbroken lineage of esoteric wisdom in the *tulkus* (reincarnated lamas) whose psychic and psychokinetic abilities were renowned. In at least one branch of Tibetan lamaism, the Nyingmapa, the lineage could be traced directly to the indigenous shamanism that had existed before Padmasambhava brought the *dharma* to Tibet in the 6th century B.C.E. The remnants of this shamanistic pre-religious tradition still existed in the Bon-po rites and practices.

Tibetan Buddhism is initiatory and esoteric, making a sharp distinction between the common folk, satisfied by prayer and ritual, and the lamas. At the turn of the century, Tibet was a strikingly religious milieu. Wherever the traveler turned he was bound to see, flapping on prayer flags or painted upon the roadside rocks, the mantra *Om Mani Padme Hum*. It was the invocation of Avalokitesvara, the *bodhisattva* of compassion, of whom the Dalai Lama was worshiped as an embodiment. Gurdjieff was undoubtedly familiar with this mantra from his knowledge of the Kalmuks of the Caucasus, adherents of the Mongolian form of Buddhism which is very closely allied with that of Tibet.

"Mountain of Merit"

For Gurdjieff, Tibet was perhaps more alien and strange than it seems to us today. The Tibetan diaspora has haphazardly spread in all directions what was once hidden. It is now common knowledge that Tibetan Buddhism is a late development of the Theravadan form, in which the goal of life is seen as the extinction into *nirvana*. In the later Mahayana forms of Ch'an and Zen, *nirvana* is compassionately deferred in order to help all sentient beings. The latest flowering is the Vajrayana, the diamond vehicle that grew in Tibet. Its rapid and efficient methods say with philosophical subtlety that *samsara* (the world of illusion) and *nirvana* (its transcendence) were one, and that therefore the very stuff of delusion and passion could be used as the building blocks of enlightenment.

The Tibetan tradition has been divided for over 1,000 years into four major sects and many minor ones. Perhaps Gurdjieff was in contact with more than one. They are somewhat different in their histories, in the initiations they practice, and in the degree to which they stress philosophy or practice. For example, the Gelupa, of which the Dalai Lama is the head, are philosophically inclined, while the Nyingmapa are oriented more toward meditation, magic and ritual. The Kargupa have a noble lineage which includes Tilopa, Marpa and Milarepa, and they teach the six yogas of Naropa which develop psychic abilities and special powers.

In Gurdjieff's time each Tibetan order had preserved intact an astounding hierarchy of yogas which were available only to those accepted into a teaching relationship with a guru, a spiritual master. The spiritual path involved accumulating a "mountain of merit" by the initial repetition of hundreds of thousands of mantras accompanied by at least 100,000 ritual prostrations. This preliminary practice could not be accomplished in fewer than two and a half months. Assuming that Gurdjieff found one or even many teachers, his stay in Tibet could not have been very brief, for it is only after completing these initial practices that the higher yogas may be approached and the extraordinary powers of mind and body known to Tibetan adepts attained.

Psychic Training Among the Lamas

That Gurdjieff held the religion of Tibet in high regard there is no doubt, for he referred to five great world religions (Buddhist, Hebrew, Christian, Mohammedan and Lamaist) in *All and Everything*.

And that he made good use of his stay in Tibet to absorb lamaist practices is also likely, for there must be a grain of truth in the possibly fanciful claim made in his last book, *Life is Real Only Then, When "I Am"*:

> For instance, the development of the power of my thoughts had been brought to such a level that by only a few hours of self-preparation I could from a distance of tens of miles kill a yak; or in twenty-four hours, could accumulate life forces of such compactness that I could in five minutes put to sleep an elephant.

Gurdjieff attributes this statement to the year 1905, and of course yaks are common only in and near Tibet.

Only a few years later Alexandra David-Neel visited various Tibetan monasteries and Lhasa itself. She found a guru and practiced diligently for many years. During this time she attained much religious understanding and great familiarity with Tibetan religious customs. With regard to attainments such as Gurdjieff described, she explained:

> The secret of the psychic training, as Tibetans conceive it, consists in developing a power of concentration of mind greatly surpassing even that of men who are, by nature, the most gifted in this respect.
>
> Mystic masters affirm that by the means of such concentration of mind, waves of energy are produced which can be used in different ways. The term "wave" is mind. I use it for clearness' sake and also because, as the reader will see, Tibetan mystics really *mean* some "currents" or "waves" of

> force. However, they merely say *shugs* or *tsal*; that is to say, "energy." That energy, they believe, is produced every time that a physical or mental action takes place.—Action of the mind, of the speech and of the body, according to the Buddhist classification.—The production of psychic phenomena depends upon the strength of that energy and the direction in which is is pointed.

Tibetans used their powers of concentration to charge objects with energy, making them accumulators to infuse the one to whom they are given with courage or make him safe. However, the less wholesome practitioner, through months of practice, might empower an object such as a dagger with the ability to kill, so that the one for whom it was intended might accidentally fall upon it when he touched it. Masters in Tibet could also use the powers of concentration to empower disciples at a distance; for example, in the ritual *wang-kor*, in which a force is placed within reach of those who know how to seize it. But as David-Neel goes on to report,

> The process is not always meant to enrich the goal to which the waves are directed. On the contrary, sometimes when reaching that goal, these waves absorb a portion of its energy. Then, returning with this subtly stolen spoil, they pour it into the "post" from which they have been sent forth, and in which they are reabsorbed.

Crowning the many levels of yoga in the Tibetan traditions are practices that could almost be called non-practices, ways of living known only to high initiates whose deep realization transcends mantras, visualizations and rituals. "The highest yogi," say the Tibetans, "is one who keeps his senses open." After the complexities of meditation practice, the Tibetan lama finds before him the vast horizon of what is called Mahamudra or Maha-Ati-Yoga, the mindful simplicity of ordinariness. Later, when Gurdjieff instructed his own pupils, he gave as a basic and all-encompassing way of living the practice of "self remembering," without retreat from the world and unsupported by previous concentrations, prayers, repetitions or theology. Self remembering resembles nothing so much as the ultimate Tibetan wisdom of Mahamudra.

> The View of Mahamudra is to add. Nothing to Mind's nature. Being mindful Of this View, without distraction, is the Essence of Practice. Of all practices, This is the supreme one. May I attain The Teaching of the View and Practice.
>
> —The Vow of Mahamudra
> by Garmapa Rangjang Dorje
> (From *Teachings of Tibetan Yoga*
> by Garma C. C. Chang, p. 32)

The Tibetan way to enlightenment is fundamentally based upon the harmonious use of body, speech and mind. Tibetan medicine is similarly oriented. In Gurdjieff's day Tibetan physicians were widely respected throughout Central Asia, and it is probable that Gurdjieff attempted to learn something of their medical wisdom while in Tibet. Later he attributed one of his sacred dances to the Temple of Medicine in Sari, Tibet, by which he probably meant the monastery of Byang-chub-gling near the holy mountain of Tsari, about 200 miles southeast of Lhasa. If this is so, Gurdjieff must have followed the great road south of Lhasa, the road used by pilgrims and by traders going to Kongnor.

It is probable that the Tibetan journey took several years and was punctuated by considerable periods of study in various monasteries. He may even have taken the monk's robe, for much later in his life the elderly Gurdjieff told a child in his company how he had once worn red robes with his left shoulder exposed in the company of others similarly dressed. On another occasion he described how he had been married in Tibet. Out of this marriage had come two sons, he said, one of whom had become an important lama. According to Gurdjieff, this son visited him in Paris, bringing an entourage of monks and making obeisances to his father. No one who was with him then has validated this story, neither has anyone flatly denied it.

Gurdjieff never said exactly how long he stayed in Tibet nor what, specifically, he learned there. But it is possible to guess at the approximate end of that period, for he did report that he was almost fatally wounded by a stray bullet about a year before the Anglo-Tibetan war. Since British troops entered Tibet on August 3, 1904, Gurdjieff must have been injured sometime in 1903. His companions managed to get him to Yanghissar in Sinkiang Province of what was then Chinese Turkestan. There he spent months in a coma. In his words, "My unfortunate physical body was able to elude destiny because near me there were five good physicians—three of European education and two specialists in Tibetan medicine—all five very sincerely devoted to me."

While Gurdjieff was away convalescing, a British force under the command of Sir Francis Younghusband invaded Tibet. The Dalai Lama fled to China, returning when the British withdrew only to find that Russia and Britain had signed a pact declaring his country free and independent. This covenant so provoked the Chinese that they in turn invaded Tibet and the Dalai Lama was forced to flee to India and British protection. Tibetan independence was not declared by the Dalai Lama in the Potala until 1912.

Meanwhile, Gurdjieff became well enough to travel again. His physicians began to go their own ways, leaving him with two companions who helped him join a caravan going westward in the direction of his family in Transcaucasia.

A Crisis

The weakened Gurdjieff waited for dawn on the morning the caravan was to leave. He pondered his life. What he saw and understood shocked him profoundly, for at one and the same moment he reviewed the actual facts of his errors and mistakes and also saw clearly what he could have done in each situation. It was as if "from one side, of a distant hollow din formed from the sounds of millions of lives of all possible outer forms and, from the other side, of an awesome silence, in me gradually rose in relation to myself a critical faculty of unprecedented strength."

He realized that although he had achieved great powers of mind, he basically had not changed. He could not "remember himself"; his mind still moved because of fears of "inner emptiness" or anticipation of gratifications. All reminders had failed. How could he keep his mind clear during every moment of his waking life?

Then he came upon it. He would renounce the special powers of mind he had acquired, and this renunciation would chafe him ceaselessly, serving as the stimulus for remembering himself. When he realized this, he leaped with joy.

When Gurdjieff returned home the Transcaucasian area was in political chaos. He undoubtedly wanted to observe the phenomena of human suggestibility at close hand. He may have participated in the fighting himself, for in 1904 he was hit by a third stray bullet in a fray between the Russian Cossacks and the Germans near the Chiatura Tunnel. A companion took his unconscious body into the wilderness where for two weeks he battled for his life in a remote cave. Well hidden high in the mountains, he slowly regained his strength until he was able to walk aided by a stick. He made his way to Ashkhabad only to find that he was listed as a suspicious character and definitely unwelcome. He limped on to Yanghissar, perhaps to seek the help of the physicians who had cured him two years earlier. After overcoming "unimaginable difficulties of every kind," Gurdjieff arrived and took up residence at the very same place where he had recovered from the previous wound.

The years between his two near-death experiences had been a time of inner upheaval for Gurdjieff and a time of profound change in him. Twice in Yanghissar he had touched new possibilities in himself which required that he renounce his considerable psychic abilities in order to develop a sustained attention in ordinary life during all his waking hours. He had found much, but he had lost much, too. Withdrawing into a Sufi *tekke*, he spent a period of two years in study.

TOWARD THE SECRET HEART OF ISLAM

> 1. Be present at every breath. Do not let your attention wander for the duration of a single breath. Remember yourself always and in all situations.
> 2. Keep your intention before you at every step you take. You wish for freedom and must never forget it.
> 3. Your journey is towards your homeland. Remember that you are travelling from the world of appearances to

Carters under the town wall of Yang-Shahr, 3 miles from Yang-hissar. These walls are typical Chinese frontier town walls, exactly like Yang-hissar's. The towns built by the Chinese were always precisely oriented according to N-S.

the World of Reality.
4. Solitude in the crowd. In all your outward activity remain inwardly free. Learn not to identify yourself with anything whatsoever.
5. Remember your Friend, i.e. God. Let the prayer (dhikr) of your tongue be the prayer of your heart (q'alb).
6. Return to God. No aim but to attain Reality.
7. Struggle with all alien thoughts. Keep your mind on what you are doing whether outwardly or inwardly.
8. Be constantly aware of the quality of the Divine Presence. Become used to recognizing the Presence of God in your heart.

Abdulhalik Gujduvani
Essence of the Teaching of the Masters

In Gurdjieff's search for evidence that the Sarmoun Brotherhood was still alive, he explored the world of Islam.

Mecca

Gurdjieff doubtless made use of his extraordinary capacity for disguise and his ability to act in order to enter Mecca and Medina, the holy cities of Islam forbidden to all infidels. He writes that with great difficulty he managed to enter Mecca in the company of some Central Asian dervishes. Following the course of all pilgrims, he would have visited the *Ka'aba* and seen the Black Stone housed therein. He also visited the tomb of the Prophet Muhammad in Medina. In his Muslim disguise he would have had to observe the laws of Islam, including the *salah*—the prayer performed five times each day at the prescribed time. The call sung by the *muezzins* invites the believers to come to prayer.

However, orthodox Islam did not provide the answers Gurdjieff considered essential. He decided, for some reason, that the living heart of Islam must exist elsewhere, "in Bokhara, where from the beginning the secret knowledge of Islam had been concentrated, this place having become its very center and source." Bokhara was the center of the Khwajagan, the Masters of Wisdom, and for their successors, the Naqshbandi Sufis. In the company of two Bokharan dervishes, Gurdjieff left Mecca for Constantinople.

Constantinople

> Men of Knowledge know how to retain the fine matters in themselves and accumulate them. Only a large accumulation of these fine matters enables a second and lighter body to be formed within man. Ordinarily, however, the matters composing man's atmosphere are constantly used up and replaced by man's inner work. Man's atmosphere does not necessarily have the shape of a sphere. It constantly changes its form. In times of strain, of threat or of danger, it becomes stretched out in the direction of the strain. Then the opposite side becomes thinner. Man's atmosphere takes up a certain space. Within the limits of this space it is attracted by the organism, but beyond a certain limit particles of the atmosphere become torn off and return no more. This can happen if the atmosphere is greatly stretched out in one direction. The same happens when a man

moves. Particles of his atmosphere . . . produce a "trail" by which a man can be traced. These particles may quickly mix with the air and dissolve, but they may also stay in place for a fairly long time. Particles of atmosphere also settle on a man's clothes, underclothes and other things belonging to him, so that a kind of track remains between them and the man.

Gurdjieff,
Views from the Real World, p. 212

Hindu masters advise the wearing of clothes made of natural fabric and sitting on a wool blanket during meditation because a person's "energy particles" called *shakti* are retained within these fabrics and can aid one in future meditations.

Early drawing of the town of Konya. Note the Mevlevi tekke in the bottom right.

Gurdjieff was still a young man when, drawn by rumors of marvels performed by dervishes, he traveled overland from the Caucasus through Turkey to Constantinople (Istanbul). The Turkish village of Konya, with its rich cultural and historic past, was on the way. Here it was a respected custom for every pilgrim to visit the tombs of dervish saints. First was Sadr al-ddin al-Qunawi, who was initiated in Sufi teachings by his stepfather, the great Andalusian Sufi master Ibn Arabi; later he linked this teaching with that of his friend Hazrati Mevlana Jelaluddin Rumi. This joining of the influence of Ibn Arabi to the Mevlevi path helped direct Rumi's thinking toward an acceptance of other spiritual paths, an attitude Gurdjieff adopted in his teachings for the West.

The tomb of Shamsi Tabriz was a short walk from that of his spiritual student, the great mystic and poet of the thirteenth century, Jelaluddin Rumi. Gurdjieff

must have seen the ceremony of the Whirling Dervishes, heard the sound of bare feet on the smooth wooden floor and the forlorn cry of the reed flute as they performed near the tomb of their founder. Because Gurdjieff was fluent in Turkish, he was surely able to discuss the holy traditions and deeper meaning of the Turn with the Mevlevi *shaikh* and his dervishes. Later Gurdjieff was to blend some of these movements into his sacred dances.

Mevlevis (Whirling Dervishes) posing in front of a tekke of Ottoman structure in Konya, Turkey.

Pir Hajji Bektash-i Veli, founder of the Bektashi Order of Dervishes.

A few hours from Konya Gurdjieff would have visited the tomb of Hajji Bektash Veli, founder of the Bektashi Order of dervishes. Here in the old Ottoman *tekke* he would have performed *dhikr* under the magnificently structured wooden ceiling, a fine example of esoteric carpentry, and later shared food cooked and stirred with paddles in huge pots. The dervishes cooked for many. It was a blessing to feed others. They were themselves like a pot of food which gave nourishment, and had to be emptied each night. Until the end of his life, Gurdjieff used cooking and the gathering at meals as a teaching situation. Years later in a small apartment in Paris he often talked to his students over exotic meals which, it was reported, sometimes included bear and camel sausages. In the *halka* (circle) of the Bektashi, Gurdjieff may have witnessed a ceremonial dance in which men and women participated, an additional influence for his own movements.

The Bektashi, based in central Turkey, was a dervish order which seems to have had a great influence on Gurdjieff. Although the rituals of the order probably began with Hajji Bektash, it is more likely that their development into the order did not occur until 1400 C.E. The Bektashi rituals included a ceremonial meal and dance. The drinking of a honey-like sherbet and the dance which included women were, along with secret instruction, an important part of the Bektashi Order. Before he died, Hajji Bektash appointed and sent *mureeds* (students) who were to carry on the teaching into different areas. Pirab Sultan, a disciple of Hajji Bektash, referred to his *mureeds* with the expression "awaken their candles" (*chirag uyandirmak*). Gurdjieff borrowed from the Bektashi as well as many other dervish orders, including the Naqshbandi, and from Christian, Zoroastrian, Buddhist, Jewish and Islamic teachings in his determination to "awaken the candles" of those who had gathered around him.

Gurdjieff once lived in the district of Pera, in the company of what he called "dervish zealots." He visited their *tekkes*, and during this stay he must have visited the Rufai Order, known as the Howling Dervishes, founded by Ahmet Rufai, nephew of the great Sufi master Abdul Qadir Jilani. In their *dhikr* circle he would have witnessed the *shaikh* perform unbelievable feats of faith, such as licking a white-hot poker, piercing his cheek with sharp skewers, opening his abdomen with a sharp knife, taking out his intestines and resting them on a plate as he chanted and danced around the room while his dervishes cried out the name of God. At the conclusion of the ceremony he would replace his intestines, push the skin of his stomach closed with his hands and show

Rufai dervish, known as the Howling Dervishes, a name given them by Westerners upon hearing their "heavy breath" repetitions.

The Galata Bridge in Istanbul, Turkey, 1913. It was from this bridge that Gurdjieff dove for coins thrown by steamer passengers.

no marks on his body. Years later, in his autobiography *Witness*, J. G. Bennett wrote of viewing a similar event among the Rufais.

Gurdjieff's apartment in Pera was close to the Mevlevi Galatahane *tekke* (the prayer lodge of the Whirling Dervishes), where he again witnessed the mystical Turn and the longing sound of the reed flute. As an invited guest of the Mevlevi *shaikh*, Gurdjieff would stand behind a small rail and view the barefoot *semazen* (turners) in their costumes of black cloak (representing a tomb), white *tennure* (dress representing a shroud) and tall, honey-colored felt hat

Pera, at Galata in Istanbul. It was in this district that Gurdjieff had an apartment.

(representing a tombstone). The musicians sat on a platform above the smooth wooden dance floor and took their guidance from the *kudumzenbashi*, the master of music. Later, while standing on the nearby Galata Bridge, Gurdjieff would ponder the sense and significance of the continuous movement of the whirling dervishes, which at first appeared to be automatic and almost unconscious. Others would later wonder in a similar manner about his own sacred dances.

In Gurdjieff's sacred dances the participants were given special clothes, similar to those given in the dervish orders. The color of a garment, its number of buttons and the manner of stitching all had significance in dervish clothes. Often the recipient of such clothes feels unworthy to receive such an honor and enters a confusion. On this the great Sufi master Abdul Qadir Gilani, in his *Futuh al-Ghaib* (Revelations of the Unseen) explains: "Then when he attains this stage and his arrival there becomes an established fact he receives the robe of honor from God and is covered with lights of honor and various kinds of favor. Then it is said to him, 'Dress yourself

Entrance to the Mevlevi Galatahane tekke in Istanbul. Photo by Nezih Uzel.

with blessings and favors and do not be ill-mannered so as to reject and discard desires because the rejection of the gifts of the king amounts to putting pressure on him and slighting his august power.' Then he becomes wrapped up in His favor and allotment without his playing any part in the matter. And before this he used to be covered in his desires and urges of the self. So it will be said to him, 'Cover yourself with the blessings and favors of God.' "

At one time, Gurdjieff was out of pocket and decided to earn some money like the local boys by diving from the Galata Bridge for coins thrown by ferry passengers. One day while diving for a few Turkish *lire* he spotted some amber *tesbih* (prayer beads) set with diamonds and garnets. He saw that it would be impossible to reach the bottom unaided because water "easily supports a living body on its surface, but resists deep descent." So he tied heavy sledgehammers to his body and retrieved the beads. Perhaps his inspiration to do this came from his memories of his father's recitations:

> Gilgamesh, I shall reveal a secret thing, it is a mystery of the gods I am telling you. There is a plant that grows under the water, it has a prickle like a thorn, like a rose; it will wound your hands, but if you succeed in taking it, then your hands will hold that which restores his lost youth to a man . . .
>
> When Gilgamesh heard this he opened the sluices so that a sweet water current might carry him out to the deepest channel; he tied heavy stones to his feet and they dragged him down to the water-bed. There he saw the plant growing; although it pricked him he took it in his hands; then he cut the heavy stones from his feet, and the sea carried him and threw him on to the shore.
>
> *The Epic of Gilgamesh*,
> translated by N.K. Sandars.
> Baltimore, Penguin Books, 1960.

Gurdjieff discovered that the beads belonged to a wealthy Pasha who resided on the Asian side of the Bosporus very near Uskudar. After returning the beads to the Pasha and turning toward the Constantinople ferry, the young man fell sick and was taken into the Pasha's house, where he was nursed by an old woman, the wife of a dervish *shaikh*. Here he met Ekim, the Pasha's son, who was to become his lifelong friend, a member of the Seekers of Truth and who, like himself, burned with an eagerness to "jump over his own knees."

When Gurdjieff was in Constantinople he usually stayed at Lubovedsky's house in the Pera district, located near his old apartment not far from the *tekkes* of the Mevlevi, Rufai and Kadiri Orders. Gurdjieff also had a dervish friend in Bursa, a journey of about five hours from Constantinople which included a two-hour ferry ride on calm waters. In Bursa he probably visited the Green Mosque and the Great Mosque, renowned for its examples of Islamic calligraphy written like murals in huge letters along every interior wall.

Dervish Teachings

Mevlana Jalal-uddin Rumi.

"Your life in this world is like a sleeper who dreams
 that he has gone to sleep.
"He thinks, 'Now I am asleep,' unaware that he is
 already in a second sleep."

Jalal-uddin Rumi

Wherever Gurdjieff traveled, from the deserts of North Africa to the remote ranges of Central Asia, he encountered dervishes. He was a frequent visitor to their *tekkes*, or prayer lodges. Among Sufis, it is customary to allow anyone "on the Path" to be a guest in a *tekke* for three days. And so, for well over a thousand years, there has existed in the Muslim world a chain of temporary refuges for seekers of the truth.

By the year 1892 Gurdjieff was convinced that he would not find in the arts or sciences what he was looking for, nor was it to be found among his contemporaries. He had tirelessly searched, penetrating various organizations, yet even with his gifts of intelligence and discernment, even after becoming a slave to his aim, he had found nothing.

"On the advice of a street barber," he was directed to a *tekke* somewhere in Central Asia. He went alone, deciding to abandon his researches for a time to reflect and reorient himself. It became clear to him during this period that the answer to his questions could only be found in the human subconscious. Many of the activities in a tekke are devoted to awakening the subconscious as well as the higher faculties in a person, and making them useful in daily life. Discussions with the *ikhwan* (dervish brotherhood) about the nature and quality of human faith and the consequences of acting by its impulse influenced his decision to stay at this *tekke* and go into a *khalwat* (seclusion) during which he meditated on the course to be taken in his life. The *khalwat* usually lasts several days within the confines of the *tekke* where one participates in the *dhikr* (remembrance of God) performed by the brotherhood. The *dhikr*, which is the remembrance of God by repeating His name, can be done either silently or aloud, in solitude or in a dervish circle, holding still or in movement. The constant repetition of "There is no God but Allah!" permeates the walls of every tekke and creates an atmosphere perceptible to the sensitive. All tekkes have holy names and sayings written in beautiful calligraphy on their walls. Gurdjieff carried this practice to the study hall at the Prieure in France, the most important center of his teaching activities.

During his stay at this tekke, and at others where he also studied at length, Gurdjieff learned the teaching of the Sufis, which some say is the heart of all religion.

The preferred meaning of the word Sufi is from *suf* (wool) referring to a small group of men who wore wool garments and were dedicated to the worship of God after the spread of worldliness. (The Prophet Muhammad mentioned that Moses wore wool clothing when God spoke to him on the mountain.)

In his writings he refers to Sufis as dervishes—from the Persian, *darweesh*, "at the sill of the door"—which was taken to mean at the sill of the door to enlightenment. Gurdjieff wished to awaken those who were still clutching the elbows of Morpheus. He often used the expressions "to awake," "to die," and "to be born." The Sufis say that it is necessary to die to everything in your life that stands in the way of God. First you must wake up to that fact, then die to all attachments. You then are reborn through *baraka*, which is the grace of the master. Although there may be doubt, the human heart knows who to trust. He understood that to penetrate the highest mysteries, he must make sacrifices and learn the ways of self mastery.

A dervish of the Sadi Order.

From Sufi masters he learned purification of the heart. All false intermediaries were to be eliminated, leaving no barriers between God and man. The dervishes taught him that the function of man is to alleviate the suffering of others. He saw that a dervish is a servant to others by means of his hands, his words, his prayers and his wealth. He was trained how to open the eyes of the heart and not to be taken by the world. This is an important Sufi teaching and is illustrated by this dervish story:

One chilly morning two horsemen were riding in the countryside. One of them was blind, and he dropped his whip. He climbed down from his horse and searched the earth with his hands. He couldn't find his whip, but found another which was more beautiful and much smoother. He climbed onto his horse and continued to ride. The man who could see asked why he had dismounted and searched the ground. The blind man said, "I lost my whip and got down to look for it, and found this beautiful whip which is longer, shinier and smoother than the one I had before."

The man who could see said, "Drop it! What you

have in your hand is a snake."

The blind man refused to drop it, saying that the man who could see was envious of his new whip. Awhile later the warmth of the day awoke the snake, which bit the blind man and poisoned him.

The Sufis say that one should listen to those who have the eyes of their hearts open, or else one can be poisoned by one's actions. If we feel love for someone, we see his magnificent qualities. If we fall out of love with him, although he has remained the same man, we no longer see these qualities. It is the heart which opens or closes our eyes. To know someone we must love him.

The eyes are the windows of the soul. It is through the sight of the shaikh that he reaches his students.

Gurdjieff sat before many such men.

There is great power and benefit in looking at a shaikh. If we have faith in the shaikh and submission towards him, then he will transform arrogance into humbleness and anger into softness.

Submission can occur after one satisfies doubt. Doubt should lead to the truth, but it is not good to stay in doubt.

There are three ways toward faith. The first is being told the way. The second is actually seeing it yourself. The third is being in it.

Gurdjieff understood that the light in the darkness is the teacher.

There is a *hadis* of the Prophet Muhammad which states, "In the body is a piece of flesh which, when good, the entire body is good; when corrupt, the entire body is corrupt. It is the heart."

The remarkable men Gurdjieff met during his journeys to often inaccessible places had the ability to appear just as ordinary village people. It is a comment on Gurdjieff and his search that so many of these hidden teachers would speak to him of that which they treasured as secret. It is said that the great Sufi master al-Junayd restricted the number of people he spoke to on Sufism to no more than twenty.

Gurdjieff departed the *tekke* and began to wander from place to place until at last he formed a plan. He liquidated his affairs and gathered all written and oral teachings on "*mehkeness*, the greater subject of hypnotism," of which he already knew much. He then set off to another dervish order, also in Central Asia, which he had previously visited.

In the 1890s, Russia and England were surveying the territories in which they had influence in order to establish a firm border between Afghanistan and India. It must have been one of these surveying parties that indicated directions to an expedition of the Seekers of the Truth which were so inaccurate that they became hopelessly lost. During their wanderings they chanced upon a very old spiritual master, a man who had rare gifts of healing. By massage he cured Vitvitskaia of a painful goiter, murmuring inaudibly as he did so, and later prescribed medications that eventually cured kidney disease and trachoma in other members of the group.

Gurdjieff discovered that this remakable *fakir* had been trained in a monastery near Kabul. With his own great interest in healing the whole person Gurdjieff must have been intensely interested in these methods. They probably came from the Naqshbandi Order of dervishes, whose practitioners attribute their healing methods to hypnotic techniques brought to Afghanistan by a family of descendants of the Prophet Muhammad himself. They call their clinics "Temples of Sleep," which suggests that there may be another root as well in Greek influence, which had considerable effect in Afghanistan during the time of Alexander the Great.

A first-person account of Sufi healing among the Naqshbandi of Afghanistan was published long after Gurdjieff's experience, yet it still retains some of the flavor of the methods used:

After the patient had been assigned a bed, he lay on his back, with his eyes fixed upon one of a number of octagonal moldings. Set in the ceiling, these moldings were embellished with a nine-pointed diagram. The chief practitioner and his assistants now visited each bed in turn. While the rest of the group maintained a chant of the syllables "Ya HOO, Ya HUKK!" the chief passed his hands, held together with the palms downward, horizontally over the patient. His hands were held about six inches above the patient's body and passed with a rhythmic movement from the eyes to the toes. The technique thus resembles that of the Mesmerists. An integral part of the proceedings was that the chief practitioner rhythmically blew upon the patient at a rate of about two breaths a second. It is this aspect of the procedure which is responsible for its name, *Chuff* (Breathing). The hypnogogic effect of this technique is probably facilitated by the relaxation of the body, the warmth of the room, the patient's concentration upon the diagram, and the occasional interruption of the light when the palms are passed across the face.

Hallaji, J. "Study of Specialized Techniques in Central Asia" in Davidson, R.W. (ed.) *Documents on Contemporary Dervish Communities*. London, Hoopoe Ltd., 1966.

The induction took between eight and 20 minutes,

A typical chaikhane in Turkey at the turn of the century. The teahouse was a common place for travellers to rest.

after which there was a half hour's wait. Then the chief practitioner went to each patient, reading his symptoms from a piece of paper and telling him that the curative *baraka* was entering into him and would cure him before he woke up. At the sound of a gong, the patients were roused and sent on their way.

In *All and Everything* Gurdjieff devotes a chapter to hypnotism.

After studying, sacred Persian charts, Gurdjieff and his friend Skridlov disguised themselves as traveling dervishes so that they could pass unmolested through small towns in Afghanistan and spend some time in the heart of Kafiristan. They hoped to find answers to questions both "psychological and archeological." On their way toward Chitral they stopped in a large town. Still disguised as dervishes they wandered through the marketplace where an old man, who had realized that they were not as they appeared, approached them and discreetly arranged a meeting. The next day they were met by another monk and invited to a monastery where "regardless of nationality, all men were respected who strove towards the One God, Creator of all nations and races without distinction."

"Not only is it impossible, even with all one's desire, to give another one's own inner understanding, formed in the course of life from the said factors, but also, as I recently established with certain brothers of our monastery, there exists a law that the quality of what is perceived by anyone when another person tells him something, either for his knowledge or his understanding, depends on the quality of the data formed in the person speaking."

These words of Father Giovanni, a member of a secret World Brotherhood, impressed Gurdjieff and Skridlov. As recounted by Gurdjieff in *Meetings With Remarkable Men*, the two travelers and Father Giovanni sat on the side of a hill on the grounds of the monastery and became deeply connected by the truth which they all sought. It was arranged that they would remain as guests of the monastery until they became clear as to which direction they would turn next in their quest. Daily conversations continued.

Professor Skridlov was so moved by the presence and nature of the monk that one day he asked him why he did not return to his native Europe and share his wisdom with other, less fortunate beings. Father Giovanni explained, "Faith cannot be given to man. Faith arises in a man and increases in its action in him not as the result of automatic learning; that is, not from any automatic ascertainment of height, breadth, thickness, form and weight, or from the perception of anything by sight, hearing, touch, smell or taste, but from understanding. Understanding is the essence obtained from information intentionally learned and from all kinds of experiences personally experienced.

"No, Professor, it is a hundred times easier, as it is said in the Gospels, 'for a camel to pass through the eye of a needle' than for anyone to give to another the understanding formed in him about anything whatsoever."

Gurdjieff and Skridlov lived in the monastery with Father Giovanni and the other monks for six months. They left, not because they lost interest, but because of the overwhelming effect that living with these beings had on their souls. They went to Tiflis, where they parted ways.

After a long time they met again for the last time, in Piatigorsk in Russia. They climbed a difficult mountain and sat in awe of the silence and beauty of nature. There, with tears in his eyes, Skridlov told Gurdjieff of the inner truth which touched his entire being and broke down his conditioning as a result of their time with Father Giovanni.

Bokhara

Gurdjieff had a special affinity for Bokhara. This region, whose chief city is also called Bokhara, is one of the oldest trade and cultural centers in central Asia. At its height, the Bokharan emirate ruled Merv, Samarkand, and Tashkent. It has traditionally been the region where the culture of China and the East mingled with the Arab and Western cultures. In the eighth century it became a major center of Islamic learning. It was natural that in Bokhara Gurdjieff should be on the trail of dervish secrets.

It was from Bokhara that the Khwajagan had a powerful influence on the rise of the Indian and Turkish empires. Many Sufis consider the Khwajagan as the source of all Sufi orders, and as such the earliest

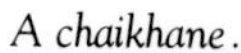

A *chaikhane*.

of all the spiritual chains of spiritual transmission. In the fourteenth century, a master of this school, Bahaudin Naqshband, came into spiritual authority. Henceforth the Khwajagan were known as Naqshbandis. The dervish Bogga-Eddin, whom Gurdjieff mentions in both *All and Everything* and *Meetings With Remarkable Men*, was probably a Naqshbandi, "Bogga-Eddin" being the Russian rendering of "Bahaudin." The Naqshbandi masters kept themselves hidden for the most part, working within the confines of whatever political and religious framework they happened to find themselves occupying. One description of these "Masters of Design" quoted in *Islamic Sufism*, by Sirdar Ikbal Ali Shah, reads:

> "This people polish the exterior of their minds and intellects with pictures, and being free from the rust and wiles of life are not of those who are captivated by the vain colorings of the world, as varied as those of the changeful chameleon; and as Naqshband drew incomparable pictures of the Divine Science, and painted figures of the Eternal Invention, which are not imperceptible, his followers are become celebrated by the title of the Naqshbandis, 'The Painters.' "
>
> (p. 99)

Gurdjieff probably suspected that the Naqshbandis, as descendents of the Khwajagan, might be able to lead him to the Sarmoun Brotherhood. Unlike other dervish orders, the Naqshbandis do not usually have *tekkes*, but live "in the world and not of it," practicing their secret recitations and employing their designs on how to live and to die consciously.

The enneagram, which Gurdjieff brought to the

Marketplace in Bokhara around the turn of the century.

Blindfolded, Gurdjieff and his friend were taken on horseback through rough mountain country for 12 days until they reached the monastery of the Sarmoun Brotherhood. It may have been within the shaded area on this map.

West and which represents man in his conscious and unconscious states, is one such design. This design is probably not Naqshbandi but Sarmoun. Both brotherhoods use various secret signs and symbols to represent their teachings, and the dhikr of both groups is held in secret. The Naqshbandis believe that teaching can take place only when time, place, and *ikhwan* (brotherhood) are appropriate. For the Naqshbandis, the vital reality of the lived moment—the dance of breath—is all.

Many aspects of Gurdjieff's Institute for the Harmonious Development of Man were modeled after the Naqshbandi order. His "work" program, study hall, duties of the kitchen and land, and the use of certain costumes for special ceremonies all show the influence of dervish customs.

Gurdjieff's old friend, the dervish Bogga-Eddin, met an elderly foreigner who was an initiate of the Sarmoun and who seemed to know a good deal about Gurdjieff. This stranger was staying in Kishlak, near New Bokhara. Gurdjieff had several long conversations with this man, and on his advice planned to visit the Sarmoun. He took Soloviev with him, a man he had cured of alcoholism through the use of hypnosis.

The Monastery of the Sarmoun Brotherhood

The pair met four Kara-Kirghiz at the ruins of Yeni-Hissar, on the banks of the Amu-Darya and rode with covered eyes for twelve days, finally arriving at a hidden valley from which rose the fortresslike monastery.

At last Gurdjieff had reached the sanctuary of the ancient school whose knowledge he had so fervently sought. There Gurdjieff was astonished to encounter his old friend Prince Lubovedsky, who described what he had renounced to enter the order and how he was to die there.

In the Women's Court they came upon a sanctuary containing ancient apparatuses—said to be 4,500 years old—made of ebony, pearl and ivory, upon which it was possible to make patterns which corresponded to postures in sacred dances. These patterns could be deciphered like documents by initiates. They watched priestesses perform these dances.

Perhaps these dances contained the knowledge that Gurdjieff had looked for so relentlessly from his youth and had wondered about since hearing as a child in his father's workshop about the ancient brotherhood of the Imastun. These dances may have embodied the truth he had hoped to find in the Valley of Izrumin, in the ruins of Egypt, Crete, and Babylon. Certainly he felt that these dances contained universal laws, truths the designers of the movements had transmitted from earlier eons. Years later, he was to teach these dances to his students. The program for the demonstration of the movements in Paris and New York in the 1920s stated: "We must remember that the ancient dance was a branch of art; and art in that early time served the purpose of higher knowledge and of religion."

In addition to learning the dances of the Sarmoun, Gurdjieff may have also acquired there the concepts of the materiality of knowledge and of universal laws—the source of the basic principles of his cosmology.

When he emerged the tide of his life had turned. He had precise understanding of the laws of human suggestibility. He had satisfied himself that he had learned all he could without going out among men to experiment. He now wanted to make direct observations. Going to Tashkent, he began to teach, to heal, to entertain as a professional hypnotist and to do business as men who are, as the masters of wisdom of the Kwajagan dictate, "in the world but not of it."

Cross and Christians, end to end, I examined. He was not on the Cross. I went to a Hindu temple, to the ancient pagoda. In none of them was there any sign. To the uplands of Herat I went, and to Kandahar. I looked. He was not on the heights or in the lowlands. Resolutely, I went to the summit of the (fabulous) mountain of Kaf. There only was the dwelling of the (legendary) Anqa bird. I went to the Ka'aba of Mecca. He was not there. I asked about him from Avicenna the philosopher. He was beyond the range of Avicenna . . . I looked into my own heart. In that, his place, I saw him. He was in no other place.

Jalaludin Rumi, in
Shah, I., *The Way of the Sufi.*
London, Cape, 1968.

APPENDIX

The Early Years of G. I. Gurdjieff
An Approximate Chronology

Note: The exact date of Gurdjieff's birth is uncertain. His passport indicated that he was born in 1877 although by his own accounts 1870 seems the closer date.

c. 1870 Born in Alexandropol to a Greek father and Armenian mother.
c. 1883 Moved with his family to Kars.
1884 Entered the Russian municipal school. Tutored by Dean Borsh and others including Bogachevsky, who later became an Essene abbot.
1888 Began to be interested in the inexplicable and the miraculous; watched a Yezidi unable to leave a magic circle, a rain ceremony in which a drought was ended after solemn prayer to a miraculous ikon, a

woman cured by a prescription given by the Holy Virgin in a dream.

Traveled to Echmiadzin, the religious center of Armenia. Visited monasteries, staying for three months as an acolyte in Sanaine.

Bought books and talked philosophy with his friend Yelov in Tiflis.

Traveled with his friend Pogossian in search of the Sarmoun Brotherhood, finding a map of "pre-sand Egypt" near Zakho.

Traveled to Constantinople where he met Ekim Bey. Returned via Konya and Hadji Bektash.

1892 Made a retreat at a dervish monastery in Central Asia.

Sent as a political envoy to Italy and Switzerland.

1895 Seekers of the Truth formed.

1896 Traveled to Crete, probably as an agent of the Ethniki Etairia. Wounded by bullet. Recuperated in the Holy Land, becoming a tour guide in Jerusalem.

Explored Egypt. As a tour guide at the Pyramids met Prince Yuri Lubovedsky, with whom he went to Thebes. Also met Professor Skridlov, with whom he followed the Coptic influence from Egypt to Abyssinia and the Sudan.

1896 Studied the newly excavated ruins of Babylon with Skridlov.

Made a pilgrimage to Mecca and Medina, returning with Bokharan dervishes to Constantinople.

Journeyed through Turkestan from Nakhichevan to Tabriz and Baghdad. Returned to Khorasan. The first expedition of the Seekers of the Truth.

1898 Searched for the remnants of early civilizations with the Seekers of the Truth, traveling from Orenburg through Sverdlovsk to Siberia.

1899 Lived in New Bokhara. Sold various wares, worked on the railway and made repairs in a number of Transcaspian and Central Asian towns: Krasnovodsk, Kizil-Arvat, Ashkhabad, Merv, Chardzhou, Bokhara, Samarkand, and Tashkent.

Stayed in Merv and from there traveled up the Amu Darya into Kafiristan in dervish disguise. Found and stayed in a monastery of a World Brotherhood.
Often went to Baku to study ancient magic with a society composed mainly of Persians.
Found a monastery of the Sarmoun Brotherhood through his friend, the dervish Bogga-Eddin. Traveled there blindfolded with his friend Soloviev. There he met Prince Yuri Lubovedsky for the first time in many years.
Explored the Gobi Desert with the Seekers of the Truth, searching for traces of a lost city. Returned to the Keriya Oasis after Soloviev's death.
1900 Met the Seekers of the Truth in Chardzhou in the Transcaspian region to prepare for a last expedition through the Pamirs into India. This trip was marked by a meeting with an extraordinary teacher and healer and a raft trip down one of the tributaries of the Kabul River. The group disbanded and Gurdjieff went on to Tibet.
1902 Wounded by a bullet in Tibet. Recovered in Yanghissar, on the edge of the Gobi Desert, attended by five physicians.
Returned to the Caucasus.
1904 Wounded again by a bullet in the region of the Chiatura Tunnel between Tiflis and Batum. Partially recovered in a wilderness hideout. Went to Yanghissar to recuperate.
1905 Spent two years in a Sufi monastery in Central Asia, studying the laws of human suggestion.
1907 Began to practice as a "healer of human vices" while continuing to study human functioning.
Became a professional hypnotist in Tashkent.
Started several businesses in Tashkent, selling them when they became profitable. These included oil wells, fisheries, restaurants and cinemas. Also instituted three large workshops for students of his ideas.
1912 Relocated his teaching activities to Moscow and St. Petersburg.

BIBLIOGRAPHY

Compiled by Walter Driscoll

These 500 entries are organized in much the same way as the author section of a library card catalog, except that material by Gurdjieff is presented first in Section I and material about him follows in Section II. In both sections, a standard bibliographic description is given of each entry. In Section I, "Works by Gurdjieff"; Part One lists his major writings chronologically with cross-references to reviews, then his literary miscellany; Part Two lists his music, both recorded and printed. Section II, "Works about Gurdjieff and his influence", lists entries alphabetically by author and then by title for the same author. Works by the same author are grouped in single spacing following the author's name. Double spacing indicates a change of author. Works for which no author is identified have been listed by title and are double spaced. Each entry about Gurdjieff is identified as a book, essay, short story, sound recording, cassette, film, etc., and then assigned to one of three categories designated I, II, or III in (parenthesis) at the end of the entry. [Square brackets] indicate information taken from outside the title page or its verso.

Category I: 195 entries. These are either devoted exclusively to Gurdjieff or bear a special relevance to the study of his ideas.

Category II: 175 entries. These contain substantial portions on, or numerous references to Gurdjieff and the development of ideas associated with him.

Category III: 138 entries. These contain peripheral references to Gurdjieff, often within the context of biographical information, critical reviews and obituaries on his major exponents, or show some influence of the ideas associated with him.

Section II also contains numerous cross-references;

these aid the user in tracking such material as biographical articles, critical essays and book reviews that relate to specific authors or titles. Because of the difficulty in obtaining periodical articles and essays, work is in progress on bringing the most valuable and relevant of these together in a collection about Gurdjieff. For the present, the reader can apply to larger public or academic libraries for periodical articles. Their inter-library loan departments can most often obtain items not in the local collection, provided one is prepared to wait from several weeks to a few months.

This material on Gurdjieff in Section II should not substitute for the experience of reading his own writings (all of which are currently in print); so before anything else, the interested reader is directed to these, particularly "Beelzebub's Tales" and then "Meetings With Remarkable Men".

In order to minimize errors and the citation of nonexistent material, over 90% of the items included have been traced, the material examined and its degree of relevance confirmed. The unexamined entries that are included have been confirmed in at least one source.

Other researchers should note that all entries cited in the cumulative annuals of the following indices under G. I. Gurdjieff between 1920 and 1977 have been traced and included:

> Bibliographic Index, Biography Index, Book Review Index, Comprehensive Index to Little Magazines, Cumulative Magazine Subject Index, Essay and General Literature Index, I.B.Z., Index to American Little Magazines, Literature in the New Yorker, New York Times Index, New York Times Obituary Index, Reader's Guide to Periodical Literature, Social Science & Humanities Index, The Times (London) Index.

Section I
Works by Gurdjieff

Gurdjieff, George Ivanovitch
or
Gurdyev, Georgy Ivanovitch
or
Gurdzhiev, Georgy Ivanovitch

January 13, 187? - October 29, 1949.

Part One-Writings

"No one interested in my writings should ever attempt to read them in any other than the intended order, in other words, he should never read anything written by me before he is already well acquainted with the earlier works."

G.I. Gurdjieff

1. *The Herald of Coming Good:* First Appeal to Contemporary Humanity. Paris: privately printed, 1933. 87 p. [reprinted] New York: Weiser, [1969]. ISBN 0-87728-048-5.

   "I consider it my duty . . . to give here the following advice: If you have not read this book entitled "The Herald of Coming Good", then thank the circumstance and do not read it."

   G.I. Gurdjieff
   3rd Series, p. 50

   Reviewed: J.T. Davis, Hound & Horn. Entry 124.

2. *All and Everything:* ten books in three series.

   "I wish to bring to the knowledge of what is called your 'pure waking consciousness' the fact that in the writings following . . . I shall expound my thoughts intentionally in such sequence and with such 'logical confrontation', that the essence of certain real notions may of themselves automatically, so to say, go from this 'waking consciousness'—which most people in their ignorance mistake for the real consciousness, but which I affirm and experimentally prove is the fictious one—into what you call the subconscious, which ought to be in my opinion the real human consciousness, and there by themselves mechanically bring about that transformation which should in general proceed in the entirety of a man and give him, from his own conscious mentation, the results he ought to have, which are proper to a man . . ."

G. I. GURDJIEFF
Beelzebub's Tales
p. 24-25.

First Series. (various editions)
A) [An *Objectively-Impartial Criticism of the Life of Man* or Beelzebub's Tales to His Grandson. Paris: privately printed, 1930.] (Provisional Mimeographed Typscript).
B) *All and Everything*: Beelzebub's Tales to His Grandson. London: Routledge & Kegan, 1950. also, New York: Harcourt Brace, 1950. also, New York: Dutton, 1964. 1238 p. (cloth).
C) *Beelzebub's Tales to His Grandson*: An Objectivity Impartial Criticisim of the Life of Man. New York: Dutton, 1973. (3 vol. paperback set) Book 1, 410p. SBN 0-525-47348-3. Book 2, 402p. SBN 0-525-47349-1. Book 3, 428p. SBN 0-525-47350-5.
D) *All and Everything* or Beelzebub's Tales to His Grandson. [Revised Edition] London: Routledge & Kegan, 1974. Book 1, 410p. Book 2, 402p. Book 3, 428p. ISBN 0-7100-1479-1 (cloth-3 separately paged books bound in one volume). ISBN 0-7100-7875-7 (3 vol. paperback set).

Note: The text of A, the privately printed first edition of "Beelzebub's Tales", is different from that of B, C and D, the later published editions. For a brief discussion of the differences, see p. 175-177 of J.G.Bennett's "Gurdjieff: Making a New World", entry 31. Although the title and pagination vary for the different editions in B, C and D; the texts are identical except that D, the revised edition, contains corrections of certain errata. For a list of these errata, an inset of a 185 word omission from page 568 of entries B, C and D, and a page correlation table for these various editions, see p.671-680 of "Guide and Index to G.I.Gurdjieff's All and Everything", entry 193.

For Analysis of "Beelzebub's Tales"
See: Bennett, J.G. "Talks on Beelzebub's Tales". Entry 41.
"Gurdjieff: Making a New World". Entry 31.
Orage, A.R. "Orage's Commentary on Beelzebub's Tales". Entries 310 & 320.
Tracol, H. "Thus Spake Beelzebub". Entry 445.

For Reviews of "Beelzebub's Tales"
See: "Gurdjieff". Manchester Guardian. Entry 195.
Kelly, G.O. in Library Journal. Entry 229.
Landau, R. "A Modern Esoteric System". Entry 244.
Raine, K. "Golden Thigh or Feet of Clay?". Entry 361.
Redman, B.R. "Beelzebub From Mars". Entry 363.
Savage, D.S. "The New Gnosticism". Entry 394
Sykes, G. "Philosophical Meanderings". Entry 422.

For Reviews of "Meetings With Remarkable Men"
see: "Fashionable Fakhr." Times Literary Supplement. Entry 143.
Fremantle, A. "Travels With A Searcher." Entry 159.
Review in The Christian Century. Entry 370.
Review in Punch. Entry 371.
Seaver, E. "Solving the Human Enigma." Entry 400.
Sussman, A. "In Search of Hidden Mysteries." Entry 420.
See also: "Meetings With Remarkable Men," the film directed by Peter Brook. Entry 274.

Third Series.
A) *Life Is Real Only Then, When "I Am"*: The Third Series of All and Everything. New York: Privately printed by E. P. Dutton & Co. for Triangle Editions Inc., © 1975. 170 p.
B) *Life is real only then, when "I am"*: All and Everything/Third Series. 2nd Edition. New York: Privately printed by E. P. Dutton for Triangle Editions Inc., © 1978. 177 p. (Contains a revised forward by Jeanne de Salzmann and the additional ten pages from the end of the final chapter of the French (Paris: 1976) edition).
Note: the Third Series may be ordered from the Gurdjieff Foundation, P.O. Box 452, Lenox Hill Station, New York, N.Y. 10021, for $10.45 a copy.

3. **Literary Miscellany.**

A) Aphorisms and Sayings.

Gurdjieff: Views From the Real World. p. 281-284, Entry 196. Contains 38 aphorisms of Gurdjieff that were inscribed on the walls of the study house at the Prieure.

Walker, K. "A Study of Gurdjieff's Teaching." Entry 467. See Chapter XIV, p.210-216, "Sayings of Gurdjieff".

B) Programs and Prospectuses.

[*Program for Demonstrations of Movement, Music and Production of Phenomena.* 1924] quoted by William Seabrook in "Witchcraft" p. 206, entry 397.

To Know—To Understand—To Be: The Science of the Harmonious Development of Man according to the method of G. I.

Gurdjieff. [Privately Printed. Tiflis and Constantinople, 1920; Paris, 1923.] A Prospectus for Gurdjieff's Institute for the Harmonious Development of Man; quoted or reproduced in part in the following:

See: Bennett, J. G. "Gurdjieff: Making a New World" p. 124-125, 127-129, 162. Entry 31.
Gurdjieff, G. I. "Herald of the Coming Good." p. 26-40.
Nott, C. S. "Teachings of Gurdjieff." p. 7 contains a reproduction of the title page. Entry 310.
Ouspensky, P. D. "In Search of the Miraculous." p. 295, 380-381. Entry 328.

[*Prospectus of a public presentation or demonstration*] The Echo of the Champs-Elysees, 1, 37. part 2, Paris; 13-25. Dec. 1923. (Periodical Article. I)

C) Recollections of Talks.

Gurdjieff: Views From the Real World. Early talks [1918-1924] as recollected by his pupils. Entry 196.

Ouspensky, P. D. *In Search of the Miraculous.* [Recollections of talks, 1915-1924] Entry 328.

D) Scenarios.

The Chiromancy of the Stock Exchange.
The Cocainists.
The Three Brothers.
The Unconscious Murder.

Unpublished manuscripts, 1924. See description and discussion in Gurdjieff's "Herald of the Coming Good," p. 41-44.

Part Two—Music

1. Recorded Music

Chants From An Essene Ritual. Piano Solos; Record IV, played by Thomas de Hartmann. [New York: Gurdjieff Foundation, © no date.]. (Sound Recording: 12", 33⅓ rpm.) See Note*

Contents: Side One, 1. Readings of Sacred Books #1.
2. Prayer and Despair #2.
3. Hymn for Easter Thursday #10.
4. Hymn to the Endless Creator.
Side Two, 1. Story of Resurrection of Christ #15.
2. Easter Hymn #17.
3. Holy Affirming, Holy Denying, Holy Reconciling.
4. Easter Night Procession #16.

From the Three New Volumes. Piano Solos; Record V [New York: Gurdjieff Foundation, © no date]. (Sound Recording: 12 ", 33⅓ rpm). See Note*

Contents: Side One, played by Karel Backer
"Seekers of Truth" nos. 1,4,5,6,13,10, 12,14,17,16.
Side Two, played by Kathy Svatek
"Journey to Inaccessable Places" nos. 3,5,2,8.
"Ritual of a Sufi Order" nos. 3,1,7,6.

[*Harmonium Music*: G. I. Gurdjieff Improvising on the Harmonium.] Five untitled pieces, recorded April 15, May 20, June 8 and Oct. 14, 1949. Unpublished. (Reel to Reel Tape.)

Journey to Inaccessible Places: [Seid Chants and Dances, from] Three Volumes (impressions of Gurdjieff's book "Meetings With Remarkable Men"). Piano Solos: Record II, played by Thomas de Hartmann. [New York: Gurdjieff Foundation, © no date]. (Sound Recording: 12″, 33⅓ rpm) See Note*
Contents: Side One, [Vol. II, nos. 5, 12, Two Seid Chants, no. 9, Baiati]
Side Two, [Vol. II, nos. 9, Seid Chant and Dance, nos. 8, 10, Kurdian Flute, no. 6, Kurd Melody from Ispahan, no. 14.]

Ritual of a Sufi Order: [Dervish Chants and Dances, from] Three Volumes (impressions of Gurdjieff's book "Meetings With Remarkable Men"). Piano Solos: Record III, played by Thomas de Hartmann. [New York: Gurdjieff Foundation, © no date]. (Sound Recording: 12″, 33⅓ rpm) See Note*
Contents: Side One, [nos. 5,7,4,1,8.]
Side Two, [nos. 3,6,9,3,10.]

Seekers After Truth:[from] Three Volumes (impressions of Gurdjieff's book "Meetings With Remarkable Men"). Piano Solos: Record I, played by Thomas de Hartmann. [New York: Gurdjieff Foundation, © no date]. (Sound Recording: 12 ″, 33⅓ rpm) See Note*.

Contents: Side One,
1. Special Reading From A Sacred Book.
2. Hymn I (Great Temple Series).
3. Hymns IV and IX (Great Temple Series).
4. Essentuki Prayer.

Side Two,
1. Religious Song.
2. Kurd Melody.
3. Holy Affirming . . .
4. Reading From a Sacred Book.
5. The Bokharian Dervish, Hajji-Asvatz-Troov.

See also:

Meetings With Remarkable Men/The film directed by Peter Brook with music by Thomas de Hartmann. Entry 274.

2. **Printed Music**

Hymns from a great temple. [arranged for piano by] Thomas de Hartmann. [New York: Gurdjieff Foundation], © 1950, 19 p., nine hymns, originally published as "Hymnes d'un grand temple. [par] G. Gurdjieff [et] Th. de Hartmann. [Paris]: Janus, [1950]. (Bound Sheet Music) See Note*

Journey to Inaccessible Places: [from] Three Volumes (impressions of Gurdjieff's book "Meetings With Remarkable Men") Volume II. Piano Solos, arranged by Thomas de Hartmann. [New York: Gurdjieff Foundation], © 1970. 23 p., nine untitled pieces. (Bound Sheet Music) See Note*

Melody for the Enneagram by G. I. G[urdjieff]. in Rodney Collin's "The Herald of Harmony," Entry 84.

Rituals of a Sufi Order: [from] Three Volumes (impressions of Gurdjieff's book "Meetings With Remarkable Men") Volume III. Piano Solos, arranged by Thomas de Hartmann. [New York: Gurdjieff Foundation], © 1970. 19 p., eight untitled pieces. (Bound Sheet Music) See Note*

Seekers of the Truth: [from] Three Volumes (impressions of Gurdjieff's book "Meetings With Remarkable Men") Volume I. Piano Solos, arranged by Thomas de Hartmann. [New York: Gurdjieff Foundation], © 1970. 40 p., nineteen untitled pieces. (Bound Sheet Music) See Note*

The Struggle of the Magicians. An unpublished ballet or review performed as part of Gurdjieff's demonstrations from as early as 1914. for descriptions,

See: Bennett, J. G. "Gurdjieff: Making a New World." p. 130. Entry 27.
"Gurdjieff: Views from the Real World". p. 5. Entry 178.
Hartmann, T. de "Our Life With Mr. Gurdjieff." p. 134. Entry 134.
Ouspensky, P. D. "In Search of the Miraculous." p. 6,10,16-17,382,383,384,386.

*Note**: Copies of these recordings and sheet music may be ordered from Mrs. Lois Bry, 123 East 63rd Street. New York, N.Y. 10021.

Section II
Works About Gurdjieff and His Influence

A.

Abdullah, Yahya

1. *New Lamps for Old.* The Hibbert Journal. Vol. 55, #216. Oct., 1956. p. 49-56. 4000 wds. (Periodical Essay. I)
2. *Alfred A. Orage Dies:* Editor and Lecturer. The New York Times. Nov. 7, 1934, p. 21. 250 wds. (Obituary. III)

Alpers, Antony

3. *Katherine Mansfield.* London: Cape, 1954, 376 p., bib., index. (Book part, p. 343-360. II)

Anderson, Margaret

4. *The Fiery Fountains:* The Autobiography, continuation and crisis to 1950. New York: Horizon Press, © 1969. 242 p., ill., ports., SBN 8180-0211-5. (Book. I)
5. *My Thirty Years' War:* The Autobiography, beginnings and battles to 1930. New York: Covici Friede, 1930. also, New York: Horizon Press, © 1969. 278 p., index, ports. SBN 8180-0210-7. (Book. III)
6. *The Strange Necessity:* The Autobiography, resolutions and reminiscence to 1969. New York: Horizon Press, 1969. 223 p., SBN 8180-0212. (Book. II)
7. *The Unknowable Gurdjieff.* London: Routledge & Kegan, © 1962. also, New York: Weiser, © 1962. 212 p. plates. ISBN 0-87728-104-1 (cloth) 0-87728-219-6 (pbk). (Book. I)

Anderson, Paul E.

8. [*Review of "Gurdjieff: Views From the Real World"*]. Library Journal, Vol. 99, #2. May 1, 1974. p. 1313. 100 wds. (Book Review. I)

Arica Institute

9. *Manual for Arica Trainers.* New York: Arica Institute, 1972. (Book. II)
10. *Arica 1978.* [A Catalog] New York: Arica Institute Inc., 1978. 71 p. color ill. (Catalog III)

Attar, Farid Ud-Din

11. *The Conference of The Birds*/Translated into English by C. S. Nott. London: Janus Press, © 1954. also, London: Routledge & Kegan, 1961. also, New York: Weiser, 1969. 147 p. ISBN

0-87728-117-3. (cloth). also, Berkely: Shambala, 1971. 147 p. ISBN 0-87773-031-8. (pbk). (Book. II)

B.

Baker, Constance Ida

12. See: L. M. Or Leslie Moore (pseudonym)
13. *Baker's Biographical Dictionary of Musicians.* New York: Schirmer, 1958. (Book part, biographical sketch of Thomas de Hartmann, p. 664. III)

Bancroft, Ann

14. *Twentieth Century Mystics and Sages.* Chicago: Regnery, © 1976. 344 p., ports., bib., ref., index. ISBN 0-8092-8407-3, (cloth) 0-8092-8148-1, (pbk). (Book part, "Gurdjieff," p. 84-102. II)

Bechhofer, C. E.

15. See: Roberts, Carl Eric Bechhofer.

Benjamin, Harry

16. *Basic Self Knowledge:* An Introduction to Esoteric Psychology, Based on the Gurdjieff System of Esoteric Development, with some References to the Writings of Krishnamurti. New York: Weiser, © 1971. 167 p. ISBN 0-87728-162-9, (pbk). (Book. I)

Bennett, John G(odolphin) (1897-1974)

17. [*Article on Gurdjieff's "Beelzebub's Tales"*] Everybody Magazine. [Nov.-Dec., 1947.]. (Periodical Article. I)
18. *Christian Mysticism and Subud.* (Book. III)
19. *Creation.* Sherborne: Coombe Springs, 141 p., gloss. (Dramatic Universe Series #3) ISBN 0-300306-41-6. (Book. II)
20. *Creative Thinking.* Sherborne: Coombe Springs. 118 p. (Book. III)
21. *The Crisis in Human Affairs.* London: Hodder & Stoughton, [1948]. 239 p. also, Sherbourne: Coombe Springs, 197?. (Book. II)
22. *Deeper Man.* /Compiled with an introduction and edited by A. G. E. Blake. London: Turnstone, © 1978. 254 p. index. ISBN 0-85500-092-9 (cloth) 0-85500-104-6 (pbk). (Book. I)
23. *The Dramatic Universe.* (4 Vol.) London: Hodder & Stoughton, 1956-1961-1966. (cloth). Also, Sherborne: Coombe Springs, 1976. (pbk). index in each volume. (Book. II)
    Contents: Vol. 1. *The Foundations of Natural Philosophy.* 534 p. ISBN 0-900306-39-4, (pbk)
    Vol. 2. *The Foundations of Moral Philosophy.* 356 p. 8ISBN 0-900306-42-4, (pbk)
    Vol. 3. *Man and His Nature.* 315 p. ISBN . 0-900306-43-2 (pbk)
    Vol. 4. *History.* 462 p. ISBN 0-900306-44-0 (pbk)

24. *Energies:* Material, Vital, Cosmic. Sherborne: Coombe Springs. (Dramatic Universe Series #4) ISBN 0-900306-00-9. (Book. II)
25. *The Enneagram.* Sherborne: Coombe Springs. 74 p. (Transformation of Man Series #2) ISBN 0-900306-17-3. (Book. I)
26. *Existence*. Sherborne: Coombe Springs. 74 p. (Dramatic Universe Series © 2) ISBN 0-900306-40-8. (Book. II)
27. *The First Liberation:* Freedom from Like and Dislike. Sherbourne: Coombe Springs, © 1976. 35 p. (The Sherborne Theme Talk Series #1) ISBN 0-900306-32-7. (Book. I)
28. *Food.* Sherborne: Coombe Springs, [1977]. 47 p. (Sherborne Theme Talk Series #4). (Book. I)
29. *Geo-Physics and Human History:* New Light on Plato's Atlantis and the Exodus. Systematics. Vol. 1, 1964. p. 127-156. ill., 10,000 wds. (Periodical Essay. II)
30. *Gurdjieff:* A Very Great Enigma. Surrey: Coombe Springs, © 1969. 70 p., maps. (Book. I)
31. *Gurdjieff:* Making a New World. London: Turnstone, © 1973. also, New York: Harper & Row, © 1973. 320 p. plates, index. ISBN 0-06-060778-5. (Book. I)
32. *Gurdjieff Today.* Sherborne: Coombe Springs, © 1974. 47 p. (Transformation of Man Series #1) ISBN 0-900306-17-3. (Book. I)
33. *Hazard.* Sherborne: Coombe Springs. 147 p. (Dramatic Universe Series #1) ISBN 0-900306-33-5. (Book. II)
34. *How We Do Things.* Sherborne: Coombe Springs. (Book. II)
35. *The Image of God in Work.* Sherborne: Coombe Springs, © 1976. 74 p. (Transformation of Man Series #4) ISBN 0-900306-27-0. (Book. I)
36. *Intimations:* Talks with John G. Bennett at Beshara./With an introduction by Rashid Hornsby. New York: Weiser, © 1975. 100 p. gloss. ISBN 0-87728-327-3. (Book. I)
37. *An Introduction to Gurdjieff's Third Series,* "Life Is Real Only Then When 'I Am'." Sherborne: Coombe Springs, © 1975. 34 p. ISBN 0-900306-21-1. (pbk) (Book. I)
38. *Is There "Life" on Earth?* An Introduction to Gurdjieff. New York: Stonehill, © 1973. 156 p. ISBN 0-88373-008-1. (Book. I)
39. *The John G. Bennett Tapes.* [Sherborne: Coombe Springs, 1977.] (Talk Tapes. I & II)
    001. Future Communities Series 1. The Sermon on the Mount.
    002. Gurdjieff—Making a New World.
    003. The Fourth Way.
    004. Human Relationships Series 1. Sex.
    005. Human Relationships Series 2. Sex.
    006. Human Relationships Series 3. Sex.
    007. Future Communities Series 2. The Master Idea of the New Epoch.

008. Future Communities Series 3. The Ideal Society.
009. Commentaries on Beelzebub 1 & 2. Purgatory 1 & 2.
010. Commentaries on Beelzebub 3. Purgatory 3
011. Commentaries on Beelzebub 4. Purgatory 4. The Two Streams of Life 1.
012. God and the Creation 1. DU Series 1. The Notion of the Transfinite. A.
013. God and the Creation 2. DU Series 2. The Notion of the Transfinite. B.
014. God and the Creation 3. DU Series 3. The Notion of the Transfinite. C.
015. To Be or Not To Be. (Public Talk)
016. God and the Creation 4. DU Series 4. Tetrad of Deity. A.
017. God and the Creation 5. DU Series 5. Tetrad of Deity. B.
018. God and the Creation 6. DU Series 6. Tetrad of Deity. C.
019. Commentaries on Beelzebub 5. The Two Streams of Life 2.
020. God and the Creation 7. A. The Demiurge, B. God, the World & the Work.
021. God and the Creation 8. A. The Tetrad of Vitality A.
022. God and the Creation 9. B. The Tetrad of Vitality B.
023. Commentaries on Beelzebub [6]. the Heropass.

40. *John G. Bennett's Essays in Systematics.* (1963-1974). (Periodical Essays. I & II) See entry 52 re. this Journal. Academy for Continuous Education: Inaugural Address. Vol. X p. 227.
The Body and Its Uses. Vol. III 127.
Cultural Streams from the Ice Age to the 21st Century. (With J. Krejci.) Vol. VIII p. 193.

A descriptive Model for Mental and Supramental Operations. Vol. IV p. 135.
The Design of the School. Vol.IV p. 289.
The Educational Challenge of the Developing Countries. Vol. VI p. 251.
The Evidence for Intelligences other than Human. Vol. IV p. 181.
Force Fields in an Organization—The Dyad. Vol. XI p. 181.
General Systematics. Vol. I p. 5.
Hyperborean Origin of Indo-European Culture. Vol. I p. 203.
Metabiology of Maurice Vernet. Vol. II p. 147.
Mind and Matter. Vol. VIII p. 193.
Outstripping Time. Vol. VI p. 50.

The Problem of Space and Time in Scientific Discourse.
(With H. Bortoft) Vol. III p. 71.
Progress and Hazard. V p. 319.
The Progress of Educational Technology.
(With A. M. Hodgson) VI p. 95.
The Psychological Basis of the Systems Integrated School.
Vol. IV p. 319.
The Specification and Assessment of Human Beings.
Vol. III p. 281.
Sufi Spiritual Techniques. Vol. VII p. 244.
Total Man. Vol. I p. 282.
Towards an Objectively Complete Language.
(With K.W. Pledge and H. Bortoft) Vol. III p. 185.
The Transformation of Man. Vol. IX p. 1.
Translation of the Masters of Wisdom in Central Asia.
(With Hasan L. Shushud) Vol. VI p. 310.
What is Time? Vol. I p. 180.

41. *John G. Bennett's Talks on Beelzebub's Tales.* /Compiled by A. G. E. Blake. Sherborne: Coombe Springs, © 1977. 147 p. Transformation of Man Series #6) ISBN 0-900306-36-X. (Book. I)
42. *Journeys in Islamic Countries.* (2 Vol.) Sherborne: Coombe Springs, 1977. ISBN 0-900306-38-6. (Book. II)
43. *Life and the Demiurge.* Sherborne: Coombe Springs. (Book. III)
44. *Long Pilgrimage:* The Life and Teaching of Shivapuri Baba. London: Hodder & Stoughton, © 1965. also, London: Turnstone, © 1975. gloss., index. ISBN 0-85500-040-6. (Book. III)
45. *The Masters of Wisdom.* London: Turnstone, © 1977. 224 p. index. ISBN 0-85500-052-X. (Book. I)
46. *Material Objects.* Sherborne: Coombe Springs. (Sherborne Theme Talk Series #2) ISBN 0-900306-34-3. (Book. II)
47. *Needs of a New Age Community.* Sherborne: Coombe Springs, 1977. 99 p. ISBN 0-900306-47-5. (Book. II)
48. *Noticing.* Sherborne: Coombe Springs. (The Sherborne Theme Talk Series #1) ISBN 0-900306-34-3. (Book. II)
49. *The Sevenfold Work.* Sherborne: Coombe Springs, © 1975. 116 p., index. (Transformation of Man Series #4) ISBN 0-900306-23-8. (Book. I)
50. *Sex.* Sherborne: Coombe Springs, © 1975. 85 p. (Transformation of Man Series #3) ISBN 0-900306-16-5. (Book. I)
51. A *Spiritual Psychology.* London: Hodder & Stoughton, © 1964. 256 p. index. also, Lakemont Ga.: C.S.A. Press, 1974, [Revised Edition] 268 p. index. ISBN 0-87707-128-4. (Book. II)
52. *Systematics:* [Journal of] the Institute for the Comparative

Study of History, Philosophy and the Sciences Ltd./Edited by John G. Bennett and Carl Schaffer. Published from June 1963 to March 1974, Vol. I to XI, at Sherborne House, Sherborne Glos. GL54 3DZ, England. (Present address of Coombe Springs Press) (Periodical. I-II-III)

53. *Systematics:* Closing Sale [Catalogue]. Sherborne: Sherborne House, 1974. An author-title index of all articles, Vol. I, June 1963 to Vol. XI, March 1974. 17 unnumbered pages. (Pamphlet. III)

54. *Transformation.* Sherborne: Coombe Springs. (Book. II)

55. *Unified Field Theory In A Curvature-free Five Dimensional Manifold.* A Royal Society Paper.

56. *Values:* An Anthology for Seekers. (Book. III)

57. *What Are We Living For?* London: Hodder & Stoughton, 1949. also, Sherborne: Coombe Springs, 1965, 1973. 167 p. (Book. I)

58. *Witness:* The Autobiography of John G. Bennett. Tucson, Ariz.: Omen Press, © 1974. 380 p., photos. ISBN 0-912358-48-3. (pbk). also, London: Turnstone, 1975. ISBN 0-855000-43-0. (pbk). (Book. I)

59. Re. *John G. Bennett*

See also: Claymont Society . . . "Prospectus." Entry 81.
Foulger, A. "A New Humanity & A New World." [An Interview with J.G. Bennett]. Entry 153.
"John Godolphin Bennett." [An Obituary]. Entry 222.
New Dimensions Foundation. "Gurdjieff" Tapes. Entry 299.

60. *Note:* Coombe Springs Press, Sherborne House, Sherborne, Glos., GL54 3DZ, England; is represented in North America by The Claymont Soc., Box 112, Charles Town, W. Virg., 25414, U.S.A.

Berkman, Sylvia

61. *Katherine Mansfield*: A Critical Study. New Haven: Yale Univ. Press, 1951. 246 p., plates, notes, bib., index. (Book part, p. 133-47. II)

Bevan, Edwyn

62. [*Letter to the Editor*: Re. entry 151] The New Statesman. Vol. 20 #517. March 10, 1923. p. 656. (Letter. I)

Blanche, Emile

63. *More Portraits of a Lifetime.*/Edited and Translated from the French by Walter Clement. London: Dent, 1939. (Book part, p. 62-70. II)

Bone, Robert

64. *Down Home*: A History of Afro-American Short Fiction from its Beginnings to the end of the Harlem Renaissance. New York:

Putnam's, 1975. 320 p. notes, bib., index. (Book part re. Jean Toomer, p. 204-238. II)

Boyd, Ernest

65. *Aesthete*: Model 1924. The American Mercury. Vol. 1 #1. Jan. 1924. p. 51-56. 4000 wds. (Periodical Essay, a parody of Gorham Munson. III)

Bragdon, Claude

66. *Merely Players.* [New York: Knopf, © 1905, 1928]. also, Freeport N.Y.: Books for Libraries Press, 1972. 215 p., index. ISBN 0-8369-2983-7. (Book part, p. 197-204, "The Romance and Mystery of Tertium Organum." III)
67. *More Lives than One.* New York: Knopf, 1938.
68. *A Primer of Higher Space*: The Fourth Dimension. Rochester, N.Y.: Manas Press, © 1913. 78 p. also, Seattle, Unicorn Bookshop, 1972. (Book. III)

Brown, Betty

69. *A Sense of Myself.* A Journal of Our Time. Number 2, 1979. Entry p. 27-28. (Periodical Essay. II)

Brown, Susan Jenkins

70. *Robber Rocks:* Letters and Memoirs of Hart Crane. Middletown, Conn.: Wesleyan Univ. Press, © 1968-1969. (Book part, p. 25. III)

Burke, Omar Michael

71. *Among the Dervishes*: An account of travels in Asia and Africa, and four years studying the Dervishes, Sufis and Fakirs, by living with them. New York: Dutton, 1975. also, Toronto: Clarke Irwin. 203 p., bib. (Book part, p. 105, 109-110. III)

Butkovsky-Hewitt, Anna

72. *With Gurdjieff in St. Petersburg and Paris.*/With the assistance of Mary Cosh and Alicia Street. New York: Weiser, © 1978. 157 p. ISBN 0-87728-387-7. (Book. I)

Butterfield, R. W.

73. *The Broken Arc*: A Study of Hart Crane. Edinburgh: Oliver & Boyd, © 1969. append., bib., indices. (Book parts re. Ouspensky, see index. III)

Byrnes, Robert T.

74. [*Letter to the editor*: regarding entry 284] Tomorrow, April 1950. p. 64. (Letter. I)

C.

Carroll, Raymond G.

75. *Gurdjieff Heads the Newest Cult, Which Harks Back to Ancient Days.* New York Evening Post. Saturday, Jan. 26, 1924. p. 12.

1000 wds. (Newspaper Article. I)

Caruso, Dorothy

76. *Dorothy Caruso*: A Personal History. New York: Hermitage House, © 1952. 191 p., plates. (Book part, p. 145-191. II)

Cavander, Kenneth

77. *To Awake, To Die, To Be Born*. Horizon. Vol. 14 #2. Spring 1972. p. 58-62. 3600 wds, photo of Gurdjieff. (Periodical Article. I)

Cavendish, Richard

78. *Encyclopedia of the Unexplained*: Magic, Occultism and Parapsychology. London: Routledge & Kegan, © 1974. 304 p., bib., index. ISBN 0-7100-7699-1. (Encyclopedia Articles, see index under "Gurdjieff." II)
79. *Chardavogne.* [A collection of excerpts from talks by Willem Nyland; illustrated with photographs taken at Chardavogne Barn, headquarters of the Institute for Religious Development.] Warwick, N.Y.: Institute for Religious Development, forthcoming Spring 1980. cloth; duotone plates. (Book. I)

Chesterman, John

80. *An Index of Possibilities*: Energy and Power. New York: Pantheon, 1974. 291 p. index. (Book parts, p. 224, 242. II)

Claymont Society for Continuous Education Inc.

81. *Prospectus of the Claymont Society School for Continuous Education.* Published annually. See entry 60 for address. (Pamphlet. II)

Collin, Rodney (Rodney Collin Smith, 1909-1956)

82. *The Christian Mystery.* Mexico City: Ediciones Sol, 1954. 24 p., ill., Litany for the Enneagram, p. [26-28]. (Pamphlet. II)
83. *Hellas*: A Spectacle with Music and Dances in four acts. Cape Town: Stourton Press, 1951. 138 p. (Book, Drama. II)
84. *The Herald of Harmony.* Mexico City: Ediciones Sol, 1954. 29 p. ill., Melody for the Enneagram by G.I.G[urdjieff] in staff lines on page tops. (Pamphlet. I)
85. *The Mirror of Light*: From the Notebooks of Rodney Collin. [Edited by Janet Collin Smith]. London: Stuart & Watkins, © 1958. 89 p. (Book. II)
86. *The Mysteries of the Seed.* [R. Collin reputed author]. Mexico City: Ediciones Sol, 1954. 47 p., ill. (Pamphlet. II)
87. *The Pyramid of Fire.* Mexico City: Ediciones Sol, 1954. (Pamphlet. II)
88. *The Theory of Celestial Influence*: Man, The Universe and Cosmic Mystery. London: Stuart & Watkins, 1954. (cloth). also, New York: Weiser, [1971]. 392 p., ill., plates, appendices, index. SBN 87728-043-6. (pbk). (Book. I)
89. *The Theory of Conscious Harmony*: from the Letters of Rodney Collin. [Edited by Janet Collin Smith]. London: Vincent

Stuart, © 1958. 212 p., Biographical note [on R. Collin], p. VII-XII. (Book. II)

90. *The Theory of Eternal Life.* Cape Town: Stourton Press, 1950. also, London: Stuart & Watkins, © 1956. 126 p., ill., plates, bib. SBN 7224-0021-7. (Book. I)

Commire, Anne

91. *Something About the Author*. (11 Vol.) Detroit: Gale Research, © 1973. index. (Book part, Vol. 4, p. 208-209 re. P.L. Travers. III)

Cooper, Susan

92. *J.B. Priestly*: Portrait of an Author. London: Heineman, © 1970. 240 p., bib. (Book parts, p. 219, 224, 229. III)

Cosgrove, John O'Hara

93. *The Academy for Souls*. Farrar & Rinehart, 1931. (Book. II)

94. A *Scientific Trail to Immortality*: Being an Attempt to Rationalize a Revelation of the Spirit. The Century Magazine. Vol. CX. June, 1925. p. 193-208. 7500 wds. (Periodical Essay. III)

Cowley, Susan Cheever

95. *The Fifth Gospel?* [A review of Philippe de Suarez' French translation of the Coptic Gospel of St. Thomas, by Susan Cheever Cowley with Scott Sullivan in Paris.] Newsweek. March 3, 1975. p. 65-66. ill. 525 wds. (Book Review. III)

Cox, Jan

96. *The Conscious Life.* Springbook Press, no date, pirated edition.

97. *Dialogues of Gurdjieff*: Vol. One, A Tropical Excursion. [Edited by Jan Cox.] 1st Edition. Atlanta Ga.: Chan Shal Imi Society, © 1976. Private first printing of 500 copies, Jan., 1979. 269 p. (Book. I)

98. *Introduction of Introductions*. Enneagram Press, 1973.

99. *Magnus Machina.* CSA Press, 1971. Forthcoming; Chan Shal Imi Society, 1979. (Book. II)

100. *That Certain Hunger.* Enneagram Press, 1969. Re. Jan Cox

101. Note: Chan Shal Imi Society; Box 14466, Atlanta Ga., 30324, USA. The Jan Cox Permanent Collection, University of Georgia Library, Athens Ga.

Crane, Hart

102. *The Letters of Hart Crane*: 1916-1932./Edited by Brom Weber. Berkeley: Univ. of Calif. Press, © 1952. 426 p., index. (Book. III)

103. *Letters of Hart Crane and His Family*./Edited by Thomas S. WM Lewis. New York: Columbia Univ. Press, © 1974. 675 p. index. (Book. III)

104. *The Creation Story Verbatim.*
See [Gold, E. J.] The Creation Story Verbatim. Entry 180.

Croyden, Margaret

105. *Filming the Saga of a Sage with Peter Brook.* [A Preview of Peter Brook's film of G.I. Gurdjieff's "Meetings With Remarkable Men."] New York Times. Sunday, Feb. 26, 1978. Sect. 2, p. 1 & 17. 2000 wds. photos. (Film Review. I)

106. *Lunatics, Lovers and Poets*: The Contemporary Experimental Theatre. New York: McGraw-Hill, © 1974. notes, bib., index. (Book part, Ch. 10, "The Achievement of Peter Brook [from 1960-1972]. III)

D

De Ropp, Robert S.

107. *Church of the Earth*: The Ecology of a Creative Community. New York: Delacorte, © 1974. also, New York: Dell, 1974. (A Delta Book) 280 p. ill. (Book. III)

108. *Conversations with Mme. Ouspensky*: 1939-1940 at Lyme. [San Francisco]: Far West Press, 1974. (Book. I)

109. *Drugs and the Mind*. New York: St. Martin's Press, © 1957. 310 p., appendix, bib., index. (Book. III)

110. *Drugs, Yoga and Psychotransformism*. in Needleman, J. (ed.) "On the Way to Self Knowledge" p. 148-181. See entry 294. (Essay in Collection. II)

111. *Farmer Clips Wings.* Wings. Jan.-Feb., 1979. p. 26 & 47. 1500 wds. (Periodical Article. II)

112. *If I Forget Thee.* New York: St. Martin's Press, © 1956. 346 p. (Book, Historical Fiction. III)

113. *Man Against Aging*. New York: St. Martin's Press, © 1960. 310 p., index, bib. (Book. III)

114. *The Master Game:* Pathways to Higher Consciousness Beyond the Drug Experience. New York: Delacorte Press, © 1968. (cloth) 252 p. appendices, index. also, New York: Dell, 197[?]. (pbk). (Book. I)

115. *Science and Salvation*. A Scientific Appraisal of Religion's Central Theme. New York: St. Martin's Press, © 1962. 308 p., bib., index. (Book. II)

116. *Sex Energy*: The Sexual Force in Man and Animals. New York: Delacorte Press, © 1969. 236 p., ill., index, ref. (Book. III)

117. Re. *R. S. De Ropp*
See also: New Dimensions Foundation. Tape #1133, "Gurdjieff." An Interview with Robert S. De Ropp et al. Entry 299.

De Salzmann, Michel

118. *Man's Ever New and Eternal Challenge*. in Needleman, J. (ed.) "On the Way to Self Knowledge." p. 54-83. See entry 294. (Essay in Collection. II)

Dass, [Baba] Ram (Richard Alpert)

119. *The Only Dance There Is.* New York: Anchor, 1974. 180 p. index. (Book. III)

Daumal, Rene

120. *Mount Analogue*: An Authentic Narrative; A Novel of Symbolically Authentic Non-Euclidean Adventures in Mountain Climbing. Translation and Introduction by Roger Shattuck with a postface by Vera Daumal. New York: Pantheon, 1960. also, San Francisco: City Lights Books, 1974. 106 p. also, Baltimore: Penguin Books, 1974. 120 p. Originally published in French by Librarie Gallimard, Paris, 1952; and in English by Vincent Stuart, London, © 1959. (Book, Fiction. I)

Daumal, Vera

121. *La Litterature*: A Propos de Gurdjieff et de Rene Daumal. La Nouvelle Revue Francaise. Octobre 1954. Tome 4, #2. p. 720-721. 600 wds. (Periodical Article. I)

Davidson, Gustave

122. *A Dictionary of Angels*: Including the Fallen Angels. New York: The Free Press, 1967. Also, London: Collier MacMillan, © 1967. (Book part re Beelzebub, p. 72. III)

Davidson, Roy Weaver

123. *Documents on Contemporary Dervish Communities*; A Symposium. London: Society for Organized Unified Research in Cultural Education, 1966. 28 p., bib., glossary. (Pamphlet, contains entry 268. III)

Davis, T. J.

124. *The Truth*. [Review of G. I. Gurdjieff's "Herald of the Coming Good."] Hound & Horn. vol. 7, #2. Jan.-Mar., 1934. p. 313-316. 1500 wds. (Book Review. I)

125. *Death of Katherine Mansfield*; A Career of Great Literary Promise. The Times (London). Fri. Jan. 12, 1923. p. 6. (Obituary. III)

126 *Dictionary of National Biography*. /Edited by L. G. Wickham. London: Oxford, 1949. (Book part re A. R. Orage, p. 659. III)

Dillard, Maybel Mayel

127. *Jean Toomer*: Herald of the Negro Renaissance. Ph.D. dissertation: Ohio Univ., 1967. (Unpublished Dissertation. III)

128. *Dr. Maurice Nicoll*. The Times (London). Sept. 1, 1953. p. 8. (Obituary. III)

Doren, H. Van

129. *The Inner Look*. [H. Van Doren reputed author] San Francisco: Centre of Inner Religion, no date. 113 p. (Book. III)

130. *Notebook of a School*. Kui Fong, 1974. 84 p. (Book. II)

131. *Silo and the Liberation*: Harangues, Dialogues and Conferences. Kui Fong, 1974. 129 p. (Book. II)

132. *Siloism*: Doctrine, practice, vocabulary./Translated by Pan-

dora. Aconcagua, 1973. 130 p., notes. (Book. II)

Drury, Nevill

133. *Don Juan, Mescalito and Modern Magic*: The Mythology of Inner Space. London: Routledge & Kegan, © 1978. 228 p., notes, bib., index. ISBN 0-7100-8582-6. (Book. III)

Dullea, Georgia

134. *Where Craftsmen Pursue Philosophy and an Almost Monastic Life*. New York Times. Aug. 5, 1975. p. 22. 1500 wds. (Newspaper Article. II)

Dylan, Bob (Robert Zimmerman)

135. [*Comments on Gurdjieff*] in Playboy Interview by Ron Rosenbaum. See entry 386.

E.

Echelbaum, Stanley

136. *Dry film of a quest for truth*. [Review of Peter Brook's film of "Meetings with Remarkable Men"] San Francisco Examiner. Friday April 27, 1979. p. 21 & 25. 450 wds., photo (Film Review. I)

Edelstein, J. M.

137. *Exuberance and Ecstasy*. [Review of Margaret Anderson's "The Fiery Fountains," "My Thirty Years' War" and "The Strange Necessity."] The New Republic. June 13, 1970. p. 19-22. 2500 wds. (Book Review. III)

Ellwood, Robert S. Jr.

138. *Religious and Spiritual Groups in Modern America*. Englewood Cliffs, N.J.: Prentice-Hall, © 1973. 334 p., bib., addresses of groups, index. ISBN 0-13-773317-8 (cloth) 0-13-773309-7 (pbk) (Book part, p. 159-168. II)

Elwell-Sutton, L. P.

139. *Sufism & Pseudo-Sufism*. Encounter (London). Vol. XLIV #5. May, 1975. p. 9-17. 5500 wds. (Periodical Essay. II)

Note: See the following letters to the editor in response to this essay.

Gurdjieff, Sufism & Pseudo-sufism: Dissenting Views. Encounter. Aug. 1975 Vol. XLV #2. p. 94-96. Letters from James Moore: Royal Asiatic Society - London, Michael Currier-Biggs: Hon. Sec. The Gurdjieff Society - London. and David Pendlebury.

Gurdjieff, Sufism & Pseudo-Sufism: Further Letters & a Reply. Encounter. Sept. 1975. Vol XLV #3. p. 90-92. Letters from Malcolm Stewart, John Pentland: The Gurdjieff Foundation - New York City, N. G. D. Choat. and Elwell-Sutton's reply.

Sufi. Encounter. Oct. 1975. Vol. XLV #4. p. 94. Letter from Ahmed Bullock.

Sufism. Encounter. Dec. 1975. vol. XLV #6. p. 93. Letters from James Webb and Desmond Stewart.

Sufi. Encounter. Jan. 1976. Vol. XLVI #1. p. 93-95. Letters from J. M. Justice and L. P. Elwell-Sutton.

Gurdjieff, Sufism & Pseudo-Sufism. Encounter. Feb. 1976. Vol. XLVI #2. p. 93. Letters from James Moore: Royal Asiatic Society - London, and L. P. Elwell-Sutton.

Frank Lloyd Wright as "Pupil." Encounter. March 1976. Vol. XLVI #3. p. 96. Letter from Sidney K. Robinson.

140. *The Eternal Search*. [Review of Rom Landau's "God Is My Adventure."] The Times (London) Literary Supplement. Thurs. Oct. 17, 1935. p. 651. (Book Review. III)

Evans, Dr. Christopher

141. *Cults of Unreason*. New York: Farrar Straus, © 1973. 258 p., index. ISBN 0-374-13324-7. (cloth). also, Panther Books, a Delta Paperback. (Book part, p. 214-224. II)

F.

---

142. *A Fashion In the Forest of Fontainebleau*. The Graphic. March 10, 1923. p. 335., 400 wds., 5 photos. (Periodical Article. I)

143. *Fashionable Fakhr.* [Review of G. I. Gurdjieff's "Meetings With Remarkable Men."] The Times (London) Literary Supplement. Friday May 3, 1963. p. 322. 600 wds. (Book Review. I)

Feild, Reshad

144. *The Last Barrier*. [A Journey through the World of Sufi Teaching] New York: Harper & Row, © 1976. 183 p. ISBN 0-06-062586-4 (pbk). (Book. II)

Fields, Rick

145. *Arica*: Inside the Metasociety. [Article on and interview with Oscar Ichazo.] The New Age Journal. Vol. II, #2. June 1976. p. 20-35. (Periodical Essay and Interview. II)

Finch, Roy M.

146. *Gurdjieff and the modern Spirit*. Systematics. Vol. I. March 1964. p. 311-322. 5000 wds. (Periodical Essay. I)

147. Forward [to C.D. King's "States of Human Consciousness"]. See Entry 237.

Fisher, Alice Poindexter

148. *The Influence of Ouspensky's "Tertium Organum" upon Jean Toomer's "Cane."* C.L.A. [College Language Association] Journal. Vol. 17, #4. June 1974. p. 504-515. notes. 3800 wds. (Periodical Essay. III)

Flanner, Janet

149. See: Genet.

Fleming, Peter

150. *Bayonets to Lhasa*: The First Full Account of the British Invasion of Tibet in 1904. London: Rupert Hart-Davis, 1961. 319 p., plates, bib., index, maps. (Book part re. Lama Dordjieff, p. 39-48. III)

151. *The Forest Philosophers*. [by C., a correspondent]. The New Statesman. *Part 1*. Vol. 20, #516. Mar. 3, 1923. p. 626-627. Letter Vol. 20, #518. Mar. 17, 1923. p. 687-688. Letter of comment by V. Rendall, Vol. 20, #519. Mar. 24, 1923. p. 719. 4500 wds, total. (Periodical Essay. I)

Foster, D.

152. *The Intelligent Universe*. Abelard-Shuman.

Foulger, Amanda

153. *A New Humanity & A New World*. [Interview with J. G. Bennett]. The New Age Journal. [Vol. 1, #12.] April 1976. p. 42-47. photos. 4500 wds. (Periodical Interview. I)

Frank, Waldo David

154. *Memoirs of Waldo Frank*. (Edited by Alan Trachtenberg. Univ. of Mass. Press, © 1973. 268 p., notes, bib., index. (Book. III)

155. *The Rediscovery of America*: An Introduction to a Philosophy of American Life. New York: Scribner's, 1929. (© 1927-1928 by The New Republic) 353 p., index, appendices. (Book part, "Notes on Method," p. 291-305. II)

156. *The Rediscovery of Man*: A Memoir and a Methodology of Modern Life. New York: George Braziller, © 1958. 491 p. index. (Book. III)

Freedland, Nat

157. *The Occult Explosion*. New York: Putnam's, © 1972. 270 p. (cloth) also, New York: Berkley, 1972. 319 p. index. (pbk). (Book part, p. 41-45 of pbk. edition. II)

Fremantle, Anne

158. *Paths to an Inner World*. [Review of K. Hulme's "Undiscovered Country."]. New York Times Book Review. Nov. 20, 1966. p. 10. 650 wds. (Book Review. II)

159. *Travels With a Searcher*. [Review of G. I. Gurdjieff's "Meetings With Remarkable Men"]. New York Times Book Review. Sept. 8, 1963. p. 10. 1200 wds. photo of Gurdjieff. (Book Review. I)

Fremantle, Christopher

160. *Ouspensky*. in "Man Myth and Magic . . ." entry 267. p. . 2092-2093. 1000 wds., photo of Ouspensky. (Encyclopedia Article. II)

Fullinwider, S. P.

161. *Jean Toomer*: Lost Generation or Negro Renaissance? Phylon: Atlanta Univ. Review of Race and Culture. Vol. 27, Winter 1966. p. 396-403. 3700 wds. (Periodical Article. II)

G.

Gage, Ann

162. *The One Work*: A Journey towards the Self. London: Stuart, © 1961. (cloth) 1977 (pbk) 139 p., bib. (Book. II)

Galbreath, Robert

163. *The History of Modern Occultism*: A Bibliographic Survey. Journal of Popular Culture. Vol. V. #3. Winter, 1971. p. 726-754. 14,000 wds. (Bibliographic Essay. III)

Gale, Zona

164. *Letter* [of Feb. 28, 1924; to the editor regarding Gurdjieff dance demonstrations.] New York Times. Mar. 3, 1924. p. 12. (Letter. I) Re. Zona Gale

See also: Kunitz, S. J. "20th Cent. Authors." p. 509-510. Entry 241.

"Zona Gale is Dead." New York Times. Entry. 507.

Garnet, A. Campbell

165. [*Review of P. D. Ouspensky's "In Search of the Miraculous."*] Annals of the American Academy of Political and Social Sciences. Vol. 268, #1. Mar. 1950. p. 248-249. 210 wds. (Book Review. I)

Genet (Janet Flanner)

166. *Letter From Paris*. [Obituary of G. I. Gurdjieff.] The New Yorker. Nov. 12, 1949. p. 90-91. 350 wds. (Obituary. I)

167. *G. I. Gurdjieff, 83, Founder of Cult*. New York Times. Monday, Oct. 31, 1949. p. 25. 350 wds. photo of Gurdjieff. (Obituary. I)

Gold, Cybele and Eugene J.

168. *Beyond Sex*. Illustrated by George Metzger. [Nevada City, Calif.]: IDHHB-Hohm Press, © 1978. 184 p. ISBN 0-89556-004-6. (Book. III)

169. *Joyous Childbirth*: Manual for Conscious Natural Childbirth. Berkeley: And/or Press, © 1977. 207 p., ill., appendices, gloss., bib., index. (Book. III)

Gold, Eugene J.

170. *The American Book of the Dead*. [1st Edition] Translated by E. J. Gold. Written by the Avatar Ueuecoyotle. [Crestline Calif.:], IDHHB, © 1974. 69 unnumbered pages, ill. (Book. II)

171. *The American Book of the Dead*. [2nd Edition] Illustrations by

Lauren Elder. San Francisco: And/or Press, © 1975. 114 p. ISBN 0-915904-12-8. [Book. II)

172. *American Book of the Dead*. Standard Revised Edition. Illustrations by George Melzger. Nevada City, Calif.: IDHHB and Doneve Designs Inc., © 1978. 144 p. ISBN 0-89556-007-0. (Book. II)

173. *Autobiography of a Sufi*. Crestline, Calif.: IDHHB, © 1977. 170 p., ill. ISBN 0-89556-000-3. (Book. II)

174. *The Avatar's Handbook*. (3 Vol.) Los Angeles: IDHHB, [1971]. ill.
Contents: [Vol. 1] Book One. Fragments of An Unknown Teaching. 97 p.
[Vol. 2] Second Series, Book One. Tales of Mother Beast or Life Is Real When I Am. 72 p.
[Vol. 3] The Prototype People. (Book. II)

175. *The Book of Sacrifices*. [By Sufi al Wahshi] Commentary by Reshad Feild. Crestline, Calif.: IDHHB, © 1974. 124 p. ill. (Book. II)

176. *A Child's Guide to Altered States of Consciousness.* Drawings by Lin Larson. Crestline, CA: [Shakti], © 1974. 23 unnumbered pages. (Pamphlet. II)

177. *A Child's Guide to Prayer*: Prayers From A Truely Great Temple. Drawings by Lin Larson. Crestline: IDHHB, © 1974. 13 p. (Pamphlet. I)

178. *A Child's Guide to the Real World*. Drawings by Lin Larson. [Crestline, CA]: IDHHB, © 1974. 18 p. (Pamphlet. II)

179. *A Child's Guide to Transubstantiation*. Crestlines, Calif.: IDHHB, © 1974. 13 p. (Pamphlet. I)

180. *The Creation Story Verbatim*: The Autobiography of God As Told to the Archangel Gabriel. [Crestline]: IDHHB, © 1973. 134 p. Limited printing of 200 copies. (Mimeographed Typescript, Fiction. I)

181. *Epitaph for An Ego*: The Sacred Dances of the Wahshi Dervishes. Produced by E. J. Gold. (Sound Recording or Cassette Tape. II)

182. *Institute for the Development of the Harmonious Human Being Inc.* (IDHHB). Box 370. Nevada City, Calif. 95959. Directed by E. J. Gold.

183. *The Joy of Sacrifice*: Secrets of the Sufi Way. [Revised edition of "The Book of Sacrifices," entry 175.] Nevada City, Calif.: IDHHB and Hohm Press, © 1978. 246 p. (Book II)

184. *Nimbus*: The Creation Story Mr. G. [Revised edition of "The Creation Story Verbatim," entry 180.] [Nèvada City, Calif.] IDHHB & Doneve Designes, © 1978. 182 p. ISBN 0-89556-008-9. (Book, Fiction. I)

185. *On Group Work*. © 1976. 11 p. no publisher (Pamphlet. I)

186. [Psyche and Essence] 20 p. No Date or Publisher. (Pamphlet. I)

187. *Tales of the Jewish Sufis*: told by Mullah Nassau Epstein. Drawings by Lin Larson. Crestline, Calif.: IDHHB, © 1973. 37 p. (Pamphlet, Fiction. III)

188. Re. E. J. Gold

See also: "Farmer Clips Wings" by R. S. De Ropp. Entry III.
"Secret Talks With Mr. G." Entry 401-402.
"Sufi Times." Entry 418.
Thatchuck, D. Interview with E. J. Gold. Entry 429.
"Wings." Entry 493.

Gordon, Mel

189. *Gurdjieff's Movement Demonstrations:* The Theatre of the Miraculous. The Drama Review. Occult and Bizarre Issue. Vol. 22 #2. June 1978. p. 32-44. 4500 wds. photos, 1 of Gurdjieff. (Periodical Essay I)

190. *Gorham Munson, Critic, Dies at 73.* New York Times. Sunday, Aug. 17, 1969. Sec.1, p. 80. (Obituary. III)

Grimsditch, Herbert B.

191. *Orage, Alfred Richard*. in "The Dictionary of National Biography." See entry 112, p. 659. (Biographical Sketch. III)

Grove, Sir George

192. *Grove's Dictionary of Music and Musicians*. (9 Vol., 5th Ed.) Edited by Eric Blom. London: MacMillan, 1954. (Book part, biographical sketch of Hartmann, Thomas de. III)

193. *Guide and Index to G.I. Gurdjieff's "All and Everything, Beelzebub's Tales to His Grandson."* Toronto: Traditional Studies Press, © 1973. 680 p. ISBN 0-919608-01-9. Includes a list of some of the errata in "All and Everything," inset of a 186 word omission from p. 568 and a page correlation table of the various editions. (Book. I)

[Gurdjieff, George Ivanovitch]

194. [*Advertisement for "The Struggle of the Magicians"*] The Voice of Moscow, mid-November, 1914.

195. *Gurdjieff.* [Review of G. I. Gurdjieff's "All and Everything" and P. D. Ouspensky's "In Search of the Miraculous."] The Manchester Guardian. April 25, 1950. p. 4. 300 wds. (Book Review. I)

196. *Gurdjieff*: Views From the Real World. Early Talks in Moscow, Essentuki, Tiflis, Berlin, London, Paris, New York and Chicago, As Recollected by His Pupils./With a forward by Jeanne De Salzmann. New York: Dutton, © 1973. 284 p. ISBN 0-525-22870-5. (cloth) 0-525-47408-0. (pbk). Includes 38 of Gurdjieff's aphorisms recorded at the Prieure, p. 281-284. (Book. I)

H.

Hahn, Emily

197. *Mabel*: A Biography of Mabel Dodge Luhan. Boston: Houghton Mifflin, 1977. 228 p., plates, index. (Book part, p. 192-193. III)

Hamilton, Hal

198. *Men of Mystery*. A television series produced and devised by Hal Hamilton, with Collin Wilson on Gurdjieff. Based on Collin Wilson's "Men of Mystery." see entry 484 (Television Program. II)

Harding, D. W.

199. *Soul Food*. [A Review of "Gurdjieff: Views from the Real World," J. G. Bennett's "Is There Life on Earth?" & "Gurdjieff: Making a New World" and P. D. Ouspensky's "Psychology of Man's Possible Evolution" & "Talks With a Devil."] The New York Review of Books. Vol. 21, #12. July 18, 1974. p. 6-7. 3000 wds. (Book Review. I)

Harrison, Catherine

200. *George Ivanovitch Gurdjieff*. The Man, his work, and its influence: A Bibliography. Library School. Wellington (New Zealand) 1976. 24 p. index. lists 89 entries with 68 of them annotated. (Unpublished Mimeographed Typescript. I)
201. *Harmonious Developer*. Time (Magazine). Mar. 24, 1930. p. 62. photo of Gurdjieff, 670 wds. (Periodical Article. I)

Hartmann, Thomas (Alexandrovitch) de (1886-1956)

202. *Five Volumes*: in memory of Gurdjieff (1949). (Impressions of talks by Gurdjieff, 1917-1928). Piano Solos. (Printed Sheet Music. I)
203. *Our Life With Mr. Gurdjieff*. New York: Cooper Square, © 1964. 130 p., map. [List of] Mr. Gurdjieff's Music, Written by Thomas de Hartmann, p. [135-136]. photos. also, Baltimore: Penguin, 1972. [Revised Edition] 134 p. ISBN 0-1400-3365-3. (Book. I)
204. Re. Thomas de Hartmann

See also: "Baker's Biographical Dictionary." Entry 13.
"Groves Dictionary of Music." Entry 192.
"Library of Congress Catalog #5." Entry 256.
"Meetings With Remarkable Men" The Film. Entry 274.
"Thomas de Hartmann" Obituary. Entry 430.
"Thomas de Hartmann" Entry 431.
"Town Hall: Music by Thomas de Hartmann." Entry 443.

Hartmann, Thomas A. de and Gurdjieff, George I. (Joint Authors)

205. *Printed and Recorded Music.* See Section 1, Part Two herein. "Works by Gurdjieff, Music."

Heynemann, Martha

206. *The Disenchantment of the Dragon*. A Journal of Our Time. Number 2, 1979. Entry 224, p. 4-24. (Periodical Essay. I)

Hisey, Lehmann

207. *Keys to Inner Space*. New York: Julian Press, © 1974. also, New York: Avon, 1975. 277 p. ISBN 0-380-00411-9. (pbk). (Book part, p. 93-102. II)

Hobson, S. G.

208. *Pilgrim to the Left:* Memoirs of a Modern Revolutionist. London: Arnold, © 1938. 303 p., index. (Book part, Ch. 13, p. 138-149, re. A.R. Orage. III)

Hobson, A. M.

209. *Birth to Adulthood*. Sherborne: Coombe Springs Press, 1965. 50 p. (Book. II)

Hodgson, A. M.

210. *Birth To Adulthood*. Surrey: Coombe Springs; 1965. 50 p. (Book. II)

Hoffman, Maud

211. *Taking the Life Cure in Gurdjieff's School:* An Intimate Description of the Russian's Institute in France Whose Aim Is the All-Round Development of Man. The New York Times. Sun. Feb. 10, 1924. Sec.7, p. 13. 2100 wds. (Newspaper Article. I)

Hormasji, Nariman

212. *Katherine Mansfield*: An Appraisal. Auckland & London: Collins, 1967. 160 p., notes. (Book part, p. 143-154. III)

Hughes, Langston

213. *The Big Sea*: An Autobiography. New York: Hill & Wang, © 1940. (American Century Series) [Reprint] 1963. (Book part, p. 241-243. "Gurdjieff in Harlem" re. Jean Toomer. III)

Hulme, Kathryn C(avarly) (1900-)

214. *The Nun's Story*. [A biography of Marie Louise Habets] Boston: Little Brown, © 1956. 339 p. (Book, Fiction. II)
215. *Undiscovered Country:* A Spiritual Adventure. Boston: Little Brown, © 1966. 306 p. (Book, Autobiography. I)
216. *We Lived As Children*. New York: Knopf, © 1938. 325 p. (Book, Autobiographical. II)

I.

Ichazo, Oscar

217. *The Human Process of Enlightenment and Freedom*: A Series of

Five Lectures. New York: Arica Institute Inc., © 1972. 120 p. color ill. (Book. II)

218. Re. *Oscar Ichazo*
See also: Fields, R. "Arica." Entry 145.
Keen, S. ". . . Conversation . . . with Oscar Ichazo." Entry 228.
Lilly, J. C. & Hart, J. E. "The Arica Training." Entry 257.
Matson, K. "Psychology Today Omnibook." p. 52-55. Entry 271.
Smith, A. "Powers of Mind." Entry 410.

219. [*Index & Guide to G.I. Gurdjieff's "All and Everything - First Series - Beelzebub's Tales to his Grandson."*/[Edited by Willem Nyland.] Warwick N.Y.: Institute For Religious Development, No Title Page or Date. Approx. 500 unnumbered pages.]. (Unbound Mimeographed Typscript. I)

220. *Into the Unknown.* [Review of P. D. Ouspensky's "In Search of the Miraculous."] New York Times Book Review Section. Nov. 27, 1949. p. 36. 210 wds. (Book Review. I)

J.

Jodorowsky, Alejandro

221. *The Holy Mountain*. U.S.A. & Mexico: Abkco Films, 1973. (Film. II)

222. *John Godolphin Bennett*. The Times (London). Dec. 18, 1974. p. 17., 500 wds. (Obituary. II)

John, K.

223. *Fishers of Men*. [Review of Rom Landau's "God is My Adventure"] The New Statesman & Nation. Sept. 28, 1935. p. 414., 800 wds. (Book Review. III)

224. A *Journal of Our Time*. Number 1, 1977. Number 2, 1979. Toronto: Traditional Studies Press, ISSN 0381-6524. (Periodical. I)

225. A *Journalist Pioneer*. [A. R. Orage] The Manchester Guardian. Wed. Nov. 7, 1934. p. 8 (Obituary III)

K.

Kafian, Adele

226. *The Last Days of Katherine Mansfield.* /Translated from the Russian by R. Bernstein. The Adelphi. Vol. 23. Oct.-Dec. 1946. p. 36-39. (Periodical Article. II)

Kazin, Alfred

227. A *Life led as a work of art*. [Review of Margaret Anderson's "My Thirty Year's War," "The Fiery Fountains" and "The Strange Necessity."] The New York Times Book Review. Aug. 16, 1970. Sect. 7. p. 1 & 29. 1400 wds. (Book Review. III)

Keen, Sam

228. *We have no desire to strengthen the ego or make it happy*: A conversation about ego destruction with Oscar Ichazo. Psychology Today. July 1973. also, Arica Institute Reprint. 5500 wds. (Periodical Interview. II)

Kelly, Grace O.

229. [*Review of G.I. Gurdjieff's "All and Everything:* Beelzebub's Tales. ."] Library Journal. March 1950. p. 400. 140 wds. (Book Review. I)

Kennan, George

230. *An Island in the Sea of History*: The Highlands of Daghestan. National Geographic. Vol. 24. #2. Oct. 1913. p. 1086-1140. photos. (Periodical Essay. III)

Kenton, Edna

231. *Book of Earths*. New York: Morrow, 1928. 290 p., plates, index, bib. (Book. II)

King, C. Daly

232. *Beyond Behaviorism:* The Future of Psychology. Grant Publications, 1927. (Book. II)
233. *Electrometric Studies of Sleep*. Journal of General Psychology. Vol. 35, 1946. p. 131-159. (Yale Univ., Ph.D. dissertation). (Periodical Essay. II)
234. *The Lockean Error in Modern Psychology.* Journal of General Psychology. Vol. 38, 1948. p. 129-138. (Periodical Essay. II)
235. *The Oragean Version*/as presented by C. Daly King. First Edition (Limited to 100 copies). New York: Manufactured by Business Photo Reproduction, © 1951. 289 p., index. (Book. I)
236. *The Psychology of Consciousness*. New York: Harcourt Brace, 1932. (Book. II)
237. *The States of Human Consciousness.*/Forward by Roy Finch. New York: University Books, 1963. 176 p., notes, index. (Book. I)
238. *The Kitchen*. Material for Thought. #7, 1977. p. 7-10. Far West Press. San Francisco. (Periodical Article. II)

Kleiner, Rick

239. *Penthouse Interview* [*with*] *Alejandro Jodorowsky*. Penthouse. Vol.4, June 1973. p. 60-64, & 127-132. 6500 wds. photo. (Periodical Interview. III)

Kohler, Mariane

240. A *L'ecole de la Sagesse*. La Table Ronde, 1961. (Book. II)

Kunitz, Stanley J.

241. *Twentieth Century Authors*: A Biographical Dictionary of Modern Literature. New York: Wilson, [1949]. (Book parts, biographical sketches of Zona Gale, Gorham Munson & P. L. Travers. III)

242. *Twentieth Century Authors.*/First Supplement. New York: Wilson, 1955. (Biographical Updates III)

L.

Landau, Rom

243. *God is My Adventure*. [London]: Nicholson & Watson, 1935. also, New York: Knopf, 1936. also, London: Faber & Faber, 1941. (cloth) also, London: Allen & Unwin, 1964. 255 p., index. (pbk). (Book part, p. 121-155. II)

244. *A Modern Esoteric System*. [Review of G. I. Gurdjieff's "All and Everything," P. D. Ouspensky's "In Search of the Miraculous" and M. Nicoll's "The New Man."] Nineteenth Century. July 1950. p. 60-63. 1900 wds. (Book Review. I)

Latimer, Margery (Mrs. Jean Toomer)

245. *Guardian Angel and other Stories*. Freeport N.Y.: Books for Libraries Press, 1971. [Reprint of 1932 edition] 308 p. (Book, Fiction. III)

246. *This Is My Body*. New York: Cape & Smith, © 1930. 351 p. (Book, Fiction. III)

Lawrence, D. H.

247. *The Collected Letters of D. H. Lawrence.*/Edited by Harry T. Moore. (2 Vol.) New York: Viking Press, 1962. 1307 p., index. (Book parts, see index re. Gurdjieff and Mabel Luhan. III)

248. *Mother and Daughter*. in The Complete Short Stories of D. H. Lawrence. (3 Vol.) London: Heinemann, 1955. 873 p. See J. Meyers, entry 279, for analysis of this story in relation to Gurdjieff and Katherine Mansfield. (Book part, Vol.3, p. 805-826. II)

Lea, F. A.

249. *The Life of John Middleton Murry*. London: Methuen, 1959. 378 p., plates, bib., ref., index. (Book part, p. 90-93. III)

Leary, Timothy

250. *The Intelligence Agents*. Culver City, CA: Peace Press, 1979. 213 p. ISBN 0-915238-23-3 (pbk). Excerpt of p. 156-158, "*The Three Functions of Intelligence As Described by G. I. Gurdjieff*" published in Playwings, Wings: The New Age Satire Magazine. Vol. 1, No. 4. March-April, 1979. p. 44-45. (Book. III)

Leavitt, Darrell

251. *A Study of the Transformation of a Gurdjieff Group*. Montreal:

Concordia University Master's Thesis, 1976. (Thesis. I)

Leblanc, Georgette

252. *La Machine A Courage*: Souvenirs./Preface de Jean Cocteau. Paris: J. B. Janin, 1947. 230 p. (Book part, p. 194-277. II). See L. Pauwels' "Gurdjieff," entry 341, p. 218-227 & p. 381-394 for English translation of parts of this entry.
253. *Souvenirs*: My Life With Maeterlinck./Translated from the French by Janet Flanner. New York: Dutton, © 1932. 352 p. photos. (Book. III)

Lefort, Rafael (Reputed to be pseudonym of Idries Shah)

254. *The Teachers of Gurdjieff*. London: Gollancz, © 1966. 157 p., index. (cloth). also, New York: Weiser, 1975. ISBN 0-87728-283-8. (pbk). (Book. I)

L.M. (Leslie Moore, pseudonym of Constance Ida Baker)

255. *Katherine Mansfield*: The Memories of L. M. London: Michael Joseph Ltd., 1971. 240 p., plates, index. (Book part, p. 205-231. II)
256. *Library of Congress Catalog* #5: Music and Phonorecords. Washington D.C.: U.S. Government Printing Office, 1948-1960. Entry under "Hartmann, Thomas de," lists printed music. (Catalog. III)

Lilly, John Cunningham

257. *The Arica Training*./With Joseph E. Hart, in "Transpersonal Psychologies," entry 426. (Essay in Collection. II)
258. *The Centre of the Cyclone*: An Autobiography of Inner Space. New York: Bantam, © 1972. (Published by arrangement with Julian Press) 236 p. (Book. II)
259. *Re. John C. Lilly*
See also: Matson, K. "Psychology Today Omnibook," p. 290-295. Entry 271.
Smith, A. "Powers of Mind," entry 410.

Logan, Anna (pseudonym? Janet (Buckley) Collin Smith reputed author)

260. *Answering Gods*; Poems by Anna Logan, Before the Gate. 68 unnumbered pages. 100 poems. (Unpublished Mimeographed Typscript. II)

Luhan, Mabel Dodge

261. *Lorenzo in Taos*. New York: Knopf, 1932. Kraus Reprint, 1969. 352 p., plates. (Book part, p. 292-307, 327. Letters to D. H. Lawrence re. Gurdjieff. III)

M.

Mairet, Philip

262. *A. R. Orage*: A Memoir. London: Dent, 1936. 132 p. Also, [Revised Edition] New York: University Books, © 1966. 140 p., index. (Book. II)

263. *Maitreya*. Shambala Publications. 1409 5th St. Berkeley, Calif., 94710. (Annual Periodical. III)

Mansfield, Katherine

264 *The Complete Stories of Katherine Mansfield*. Auckland: Golden Press, 1974. 830 p. (New Zealand Classics Giant) ISBN 0-8558-261-8. (cloth). (Book, Fiction. III)

265. *The Letters of Katherine Mansfield*./Edited by J. Middleton Murry (2 Vol.) London: Constable, 1928. (Book part, Vol. 2 p. 259-268. II)

266. Re. *Katherine Mansfield*
See also: Alpers, A. "Katherine Mansfield." Entry 3.
Berkman, S. "Katherine Mansfield." Entry 61.
Hormasji, N. "Katherine Mansfield." Entry 212.
Kafian, A. "Last Days of Katherine Mansfield." Entry 226.
Lawrence, D. Y. "Collected Letters." Entry 247.
Lea, F. A. "Life of J. M. Murry." Entry 249.
L. M. "Katherine Mansfield." Entry 255.
Meyers, J. "Mansfield, Gurdjieff & Lawrence's. . . ." Entry 279.
Orage, A.R. "Talks with Katherine Mansfield." Entry 322.
Wright, O. "Last Days of Katherine Mansfield." Entry 500.

Marshall-Cavindish

267. *Man, Myth and Magic*: An illustrated Encyclopedia of the Supernatural. London: Parnell, © 1970, 1971. 3157 p. [originally published as a weekly serial in 111 issues]. Articles on Gurdjieff and P. D. Ouspensky, see entries 160 & 448. (Encyclopedia Articles, p. 1188-1189, 2092-2093. II)

Martin, Desmond R.

268. *Below the Hindu Kush.* The Lady (London). Vol. 162 #4210. Dec. 9, 1965. p. 870. 1500 wds. Also published as "Account of the Sarmoun Brotherhood" in "Contemporary Dervish Communities," entry 123, p. 22-24, 1400 wds., edited version. (Periodical Article. I)

Martin, Wallace

269. *The New Age under Orage*: Chapters in English cultural history. Manchester Univ. Press, © 1967. 303 p. (Book. III)

270. *Material For Thought*. Far West Press. Box 549. San Francisco. Calif. 94101. (Annual Periodical. II)

Matson, Katinka

271. *The Psychology Today Omnibook of Personal Development*. New York: Morrow, © 1977. 500 p. ISBN 0-688-03225-7. Biographical sketches of G. I. Gurdjieff, O. Ichazo, J. Lilly, C. Naranjo, R. Ornstein, P. D. Ouspensky, C. Tart, and many others. (Book parts. II)

Matthiessen, Peter

272. *The Snow Leopard*. New York: Viking, © 1978. 338 p., index,

notes, ref. (Book part, p. 43. III)

Meaker, Jack

273. *My Meager Tale.* Sherborne: Coombe Springs Press, [1977]. 132 p. (Book. II)

274. *Meetings With Remarkable Men.*/A Remar Production. New York: Libra Films, 1979. 2 hrs. Directed by Peter Brook. Starring Dragan Maksimovic (as Gurdjieff), Ter ence Stamp and Warren Mitchell. Produced by Stuart Lyons. Screenplay by Jeanne de Salzmann and Peter Brook based on the book by G. I. Gurdjieff. Music by Thomas de Hartmann and Laurence Rosenthal. Photography by Gilbert Taylor. Note: Remar Productions. 50 Rockefeller Plaza, New York, 10020 N.Y. Libra Film Distributors. 150 E. 58th St. New York City. (Film. I)
Reviewed in: Croyden M. "Filming the Saga of a Sage." Entry 105.
Echelbaum, S. "Dry film of a quest for truth." Entry 136.
"Meetings With Remarkable Men" A Journal of Our Time, #2. Entry 175.
Parabola. "Leaning on the Moment." Entry 339.
Travers, P. L. "Meetings With Remarkable Men." Entry 449.

275. *Meetings With Remarkable Men—A Film.* A Journal of Our Time. Number 2, 1979. p. 81. 200 wds. (Film Review. I)

276. *Men, Masters & Messiahs.* Time (Magazine). p. 20, 1936. p. 34-40., photo of Gurdjieff, 2400 wds. (Periodical Article. I)

Metzner, Ralph

277. [*Review of Kenneth Walker's "The Making of Man."*] The Psychedelic Review. Vol. 1 #4, 1964. p. 485-486. 700 wds. (Book Review. II)

278. [*Review of C. D. King's "The States of Human Consciousness"*] The Psychedelic Review. Vol. 1 #4, 1964. p. 486-489. 1600 wds. (Book Review. II)

Meyers, Jeffery

279. *Katherine Mansfield, Gurdjieff and Lawrence's "Mother and Daughter."* Twentieth Century Literature. Vol. 22. Dec. 1976. p. 444-453. 4200 wds. An analysis of entry 248. (Periodical Essay. II)

280. *Mr. A. R. Orage.* The Times (London). Wed. Nov. 7, 1934. 375 wds. (Obituary. III)

281. *Mr. George Gurdjieff.* The Times (London) Nov. 12, 1949. 7e & 5. 250 wds. (Obituary. I)

Moorehead, Joseph H. Jr.

282. *George I. Gurdjieff*: A bibliography. Bulletin of Bibliography. Vol. 28 #4. Oct.-Dec., 1971. p. 117-118. Lists 45 items. (Bibliography. I)

Morley, Christopher

283. *Inward Ho!* New York: Doubleday, 1923. (Book part, p. 55-67, "Fontainebleau and Vesey Street." II)

Munson, Gorham Bert

284. *Black Sheep Philosophers*: Gurdjieff-Ouspensky-Orage. Tomorrow. Vol.9 #6. Feb. 1950. p. 20-25. 5000 wds. (Periodical Essay. I) See also: R. T. Byrnes "Letter to the editor," entry 74, regarding this essay.

285. *Mankind Asleep in a Prison*. [Review of P. D. Ouspensky's "In Search of the Miraculous."] The Saturday Review of Literature. Aug. 19, 1950. p. 17. 750 wds. (Book Review. I)

286. *Orage In America*. Dynamic America. Vol. 10. [Part 1], May 1940, p. 17-20. [Part 2], June 1940, p. 12-16. 7000 wds. (Biographical Periodical Essay. I)

287. *The Significançe of Jean Toomer*. Opportunity. Vol. 3. Sept., 1925. p. 262-263. 2000 wds. (Periodical Article. III)

288. Re. *Gorham Munson*

See also: Boyd, E. "Aesthete: Model 1924. Entry 65.
"Gorham Munson Dies." New York Times. 190.
Kunitz, S. J. "Twentieth Century Authors." Entry 441 & 242.

N.

Naranjo, Claudio

289. *The One Quest*. New York: Viking Press, 1972. (Esalen Book)

290. Re. Claudio Naranjo

See also: Matson, K. "Psychology Today Omni Book," p. 342-345. Entry 271.

Naumburg, Margaret

291. *The Child and the World*: Dialogues in Modern Education. New York: Harcourt Brace, © 1928. 328 p., bib. (Book. II)

Needleman, Jacob

292. *The New Religions*. New York: Doubleday, 1970. (Book part, p. 208-211. II)

293. *A Note On Gurdjieff's Ideas*. Maitreya. Vol. [1, 1970]. p. 16-18. 1000 wds. (Periodical Essay. I)

294. *On The Way To Self Knowledge*./Edited by Jacob Needleman & Dennis Lewis. New York: Knopf, © 1976. 241 p., photos. ISBN 0-394-49753-8, (cloth). 0-394-73280-4, (pbk). Includes entries 110 & 118. (Book, Essays in Collection. II)

295. *Sacred Tradition and Present Need*./Edited by Jacob Needleman & Dennis Lewis. New York: Viking, © 1975. (An Eslan Book). 146 p. ISBN 0-670-61441-6. Includes entries 378 & 450 (Book, Essays in Collection. II)

296. *A Sense of the Cosmos*: The Encounter of Modern Science and Ancient Truth. Garden City, N.Y.: Doubleday, © 1975. 178 p., bib., ref., index. (Book. III)

297. *Understanding the New Religions*./Edited by Jacob Needleman and George Baker. New York: Seabury Press, © 1978. (A Crossroad Book) 314 p., notes, bib., index. ISBN 0-8164-0403-8 (cloth) 0-8164-2188-9 (pbk). (Book. III)

298. *The New Cult of Gurdjieff*: An Effort to Realize "Cosmic Consciousness." Current Opinion. Vol. 76. April 1924 p. 467-468. Photo of Gurdjieff. (Periodical Article. I)

New Dimensions Foundation

299. *Gurdjieff*. [Tape Set] #1133. Interview on K.Q.E.D. F.M., San Francisco by [Larry Guise & Robert Lockland] of Robert De Ropp, Kathleen R. Speeth and Charles Tart regarding the Gurdjieff Work. Includes excerpts of tapes of talks by John G. Bennett and music composed and played by G. I. Gurdjieff. (4 × 60 min. Cassette Tapes. I)

Nicoll, (Henry) Maurice (Dunlop) (1884-1953)

300. *The Idea of Transformation in the Work*: [An excerpt from "Psychological Commentaries . . ." Vol. 1, p. 50-55. See entry 305.] Maitreya #3. Berkeley: Shambala, © 1972. (Book part published as a Periodical Article. I)

301. *Living Time*: and the Integration of the Life. London: Watkins, © 1952. 252 p., bib., index. also, 1976, ISBN 0-7224-0146-9 (pbk). (Book. II)

302. *The Mark*. London: Stuart & Watkins, 1954. 216 p. appendix, index. SBN 7224-0061-6. (Book. II)

303. *The New Man*: An Interpretation of Some Parables and Miracles of Christ. London: Stuart & Richards, 1950. also, London: Stuart, 1955. also, London: Robinson & Watkins, © 1967. 153 p. SBN 7224-0000-4 (cloth). also, Harmondsworth: Penguin, 1972. 184 p. (pbk) (Book. I)

304. *On the Formation of a Psychological Body*. [An excerpt from "Psychological Commentaries . . ." Vol. 4, p. 1384-1385. See entry 305.] Maitreya #6. Berkeley: Shambala, 1977. p. 21-[23]. (Book part published as a Periodical Article. I)

305. *Psychological Commentaries*: On the Teaching of G. I. Gurdjieff and P. D. Ouspensky. (5 Vol.) London: Vincent Stuart, Vol. 1-2-3, 1954, 1964. Vol. 4. SBN 7224-0066-7. and Vol. 5. SBN 7224-0067-3, 1966, 1968. 1766 p. (Book. I)

306. Re. *Maurice Nicoll*

See also: "Dr. Maurice Nicoll." The Times, Obituary. Entry 128.

Pogson, B. "Maurice Nicoll: A Portrait." Entry 351.

Swayne, Martin (pseudonym of Maurice Nicoll). "The Blue Germ." Entry 421.

307. *Nimbus:* The Creation Story According to Mr. G. See: [E. J. Gold], "Nimbus: The Creation Story . . ." Entry 184.

Norelli-Bachelet, Patrizia

308. *The Gnostic Circle:* a synthesis in the harmonies of the cosmos. Panorama City, Calif.: Aeon Books, © 1975. (Book part, p. 123-126. III)

Nott, C. S.

309. *Journey Through This World*: The Second Journal of a Pupil, Including an account of meetings with G. I. Gurdjieff, A. R. Orage and P. D. Ouspensky. New York: Weiser, © 1969. 254 p. index. Also published with altered title as *Further Teachings of Gurdjieff*: Journey through this world. New York: Weiser, [1978]. 254 p. index. ISBN 0-87728-105-X (cloth). 0-87728-396-6 (pbk). (Book. I)

310. *Teachings of Gurdjieff:* The Journal of a Pupil, An Account of Some Years with G. I. Gurdjieff and A. R. Orage in New York and at the Fontainebleau-Avon New York: Weiss, 1962: 230 p., index. ISBN 0-87728-106-8, (cloth). 0-87728-395-8. (pbk., 1978).

Note: Chapter 3, p. 125-215, [A. R.] "Orage's Commentary on 'Beelzebub'." (Book. I)

Nyland, Willem A. (1890-1975)

311. *Firefly.* First Part. 83 p. Second Part. 113 p. (Privately printed and Distributed). [Warwick, N.Y.: Institute for Religious Development, no date, 196?.] (Unbound Mimeographed Typescript. I)

Firefly. Third Part. (Incomplete Unpublished Manuscript. I)

312. [*Piano and Organ Music*.]Warwick N.Y.: Gage Hill Press. 196?-197?. (Various Untitled reel to reel tapes and sound recordings. II)

313. *Talk Tapes*. Warwick N.Y.: Institute for Religious Development. A Series of Untitled 90 min. cassette tapes and typed transcriptions of talks by and with W. Nyland between 195? and 1975. Privately Distributed. (Cassette Tapes and Typescripts. I)

314. Re. *Willem Nyland*

See also: "Chardavogne." Entry 79.
"Index and Guide to . . . Beelzebub's Tales." Entry 219.

O.

Orage, Alfred Richard (1873-1934)

315. *The Active Mind*: Adventures in Awareness. [Janus Press, 1930]. also, New York: Hermitage House, 1954. [Revised Edi-

tion] Published as *The Active Mind*: Psychological Exercises & Essays. New York: Weiser, 1965. 121 p. (cloth). also, New York: Weiser, 1974. ISBN 0-87728-265-X (pbk). (Book. I)

316. *Consciousness*: Animal, Human and Superhuman. New York: Weiser, 1974. 86 p. ISBN 0-87728-251-X (pbk). (Book. III)

317. *An Editor's Progress.* The Commonweal. Vol. 3, 1926.
Part I. "The New Age." Feb. 10, 1926. p. 376-379.
Part II. "The Douglas Revelation." Feb. 17, 1926.
Part III. "The Impossibility of Reform." Feb. 24, 1926. p. 434-435.
Part IV. "The Quest of God." Mar. 3, 1926. p. 456-457.
7000 wds. (Autobiographical Periodical Essay. II)

318. *On Love*: With Some Aphorisms & Other Essays [Including a Biographical Note & a short Bibliography]. New York: Weiser, 1966. 72 p. (cloth). also, 1974, LSBN 0-87728-264-1. (Book. I)

319. *Orage As Critic.*/Edited with an introduction by Wallace Martin, London: Routledge & Kegan, © 1974. 218 p., bib., index. (Book. III)

320. *Orage's Commentary on Beelzebub.* See C. S. Nott's "Teachings of Gurdjieff," p. 125-215. Entry 310.

321. *Selected Essays & Critical Writings.*/Edited by Herbert Reed & Denis Saurat. Freeport, N.Y.: Books for Libraries Press, 1967. © 1935. 216 p. (Book. II)

322. *Talks with Katherine Mansfield.* The Century Illustrated Monthly Magazine. Nov. 1924. p. 36-40. Also published in "Selected Essays & Critical Writings." Entry 321. (Periodical Article. II)

323. Re. A. *R. Orage*
See also: "Alfred R. Orage Dies." New York Times. Entry 2.
"Dictionary of National Biography," p. 659. Entry 126.
Gurdjieff, G. I. "Life is real only then, when 'I Am'."
Hobson, S. G. "Pilgrim to the Left." Entry 208.
"A Journalist Pioneer." Manchester Guardian. Entry 225.
King, C. D. "The Oragean Version." Entry 235.
Mairet P. "A. R. Orage: A Memoir." Entry 262.
Martin, Wallace. A. *R. Orage*: [An In Depth Bibliography]. Forthcoming in English Literature in Transition. Announced as "in progress or completed" in Vol. 18 #1, 1975, p. 50.
"Mr. A. R. Orage." Times (London) Obituary. Entry 280.
Munson, G. "Orage in America." Entry 286.
Selver, P. "Orage and the New Age Circle." Entry 403.

Ornstein, Robert Evans

324. *The Psychology of Consciousness*. San Francisco: Freeman, 1972. 347 p., notes, index. (Book. III)

325. Re. *R. E. Ornstein*
See also: biographical sketch in K. Matson's "Psychology Today Omnibook." p. 352-356. Entry 271.

Osborn, Arthur W.

326. *The Axis and the Rim*: The Quest For Reality In A Modern Setting. London: Vincent Stuart, 1963. 203 p., bib., index. (Book. III)

Ouspensky, Peter Demianovitch (1878-1947)
Ouspensky, Pytor Demianovitch
Uspenskii, Petr Demianovich

327. *The Fourth Way*: A Record of Talks and Answers to Questions based on the teaching of G. I. Gurdjieff. New York: Knopf, 1957. (cloth). also, New York: Random House, 1971. (Vintage Books). 446 p., index. (pbk). (Book I)

328. *In Search of the Miraculous*: Fragments of an Unknown Teaching. New York: Harcourt Brace & World, © 1949. 399 p., index. (cloth). also, New York: Harcourt Brace & World, 196?. (Vintage Books), ISBN 0-15-644508-5, (pbk). (Book. I)
Reviewed in:
Garnet A. C. Entry 165.
"Gurdjieff" in Manchester Guardian. Entry 195.
"Into the Unknown," New York Times. Entry 220.
Landau, R. "A Modern Esoteric System." Entry 244.
Munson, G. "Mankind Asleep In Prison." Entry 285.
"Ouspensky's System." Times (London). Entry 337.
Raine, K. "Golden Thigh or Feet of Clay." Entry 361.
Savage, D. S. "New Gnosticism." Entry 394.
Sugrue, T. "Pursuit of Esoteric Lore." Entry 419.

329. *Letters from Russia*: 1919. London: Routledge & Kegan, L978. (Book. III)

330. A *New Model of the Universe*: Principles of the Psychological Method in its Application to Problems of Science, Religion and Art. London: Routledge & Kegan, 1st Edition 1931. 2nd Ed. 1934, 3rd Ed. 1938. 554 p., index. also, New York: Random House, 1971. (Vintage Books) ISBN 0-394-71524-1, (pbk). (Book. II)

331. *The Psychology of Man's Possible Evolution*. [London]: Hedgehog Press, © 1950. also, London: Hodder & Stoughton, 1951. 95 p., index. also, New York: Knopf, 1954. also, Knopf, 1974, *2nd Enlarged Edition* [With Autobiographical Note], 128 p. ISBN 0-394-48755-9, (cloth). also, New York: Random, 1974. 128 p. (Vintage Books), ISBN 0-394-71943-3, (pbk). (Book. I)

332. *Strange Life of Ivan Osokin*: A Novel. New York: Holme Press, © 1947. also, London: Stourton Press, 1947. also, London: Faber & Faber, 1948. also, New York: Hermitage House, 1955. 166 p. [Originally published in Russia (1915) as "Kinemadrama."] (Book, Fiction. II)

333. *Talks With A Devil.*/ Translated by Katya Petroff. Edited and introduced by John G. Bennett. London: Turnstone, © 1972. [First Published in St. Petersburg, 1916]. 155 p. ISBN 0-85500-004-X. (Book. III)

334. *Tertium Organum*: The Third Canon of Thought, A key to the Enigmas of the World./ Translated From the Russian by Nicholas Bessaraboff and Claude Bragdon, with an Introduction by Claude Bragdon, Rochester N.Y.: Manas Press, © 1920. also, New York: Knopf, 1st Edition 1920, 2nd Edition 1922, 3rd Edition 1945. 306 p. also, London: Paul, Trench & Trubner, 1934. also, Capetown: Stourton Press, 1950. Translated by E. Kadloubovsky under the author's supervision. also, New York: Ràndom, 197?. (pbk). (Book. III)

335. Re. *P. D. Ouspensky*

See also: Bragdon, C. "Merely Players." p. 197-204. Entry 66.
Fisher, A. P. "The Influence of Ouspensky's 'Tertium Organum'. . ." Entry 148.
Fremantle, C. "Ouspensky." Entry 160.
Landau, R. "God Is My Adventure," Chapter VIII "War Against Sleep: P. D. Ouspensky," p. 121-136. Unwin Edition. Entry 243.
Matson, K. "Psychology Today Omnibook" p. 356-360. Entry 271.
Nott, C. S. "Journey Through This World." Entry 309.
"Remembering Pyotr Demianovich Ouspensky." Entry 366.
Tedlock, E. W. "D. H. Lawrence's Annotations of Ouspensky . . ." Entry 428.

336. [*Ouspensky, P. D.*] The Times (London), Nov. 5, 1947. p.7. (Listed in the Times Index but not included in the microfilmed edition). (Obituary. III)

337. *Ouspensky's System*. [Review of P. D. Ouspensky's "In Search of the Miraculous"] The Times Literary Supplement (London). May 26, 1950. p.328. 1200 wds. (Book Review. I)

338. *Parabola.*/ Edited by D. M. Dooling. New York: Society for the Study of Myth and Tradition. Quarterly since 1976. Contains several articles by P. L. Travers (a contributing editor), Jacob Needleman with occasional contributions from Christopher Fremantle, Lizelle Reymond and Jean Toomer. (Periodical. III)

P.

Parabola

339. *Leaning on the Moment*: A Conversation with Peter Brook. Parabola: Myth and the Quest for Meaning, Sacred Dance Issue. Vol. IV # 2, May 1979. p. 46-59. See p. 54-59 for discussion of and stills from Brook's film of Gurdjieff's "Meetings With Remarkable Men." (Periodical Interview. I)

Parker, Claude

340. [*Review of J. G. Bennett's "Gurdjieff: Making a New World*."] Library Journal. April 1, 1974. p. 1041. 125 wds. (Book Review. II)

Pauwels, Louis

341. *Gurdjieff*. Douglas, Isle of Man: Times Press, © 1964. also, New York: Weiser, 1972. ISBN 0-87728-1785, (pbk). First published as "Monsieur Gurdjieff: Documents, temoignages, texts et commentaires sur un societe contemporaine." Paris: Editions du Seuil, 1954. (Book. I)
Reviewed in:
Rees, R. "For Love or Money." Entry 364.
Regamey, P. R. "Monsieur Gurdjieff." Entry 365.
Williams, S. "Gurdjieff Through Many Eyes." Entry 482.
"Wisdom Through Mystification." Entry 494.

Pauwels, Louis & Bergier, Jacques

342. *The Morning of the Magicians*./ Translated by Rollo Myers. New York: Avon, 1968. 416 p. (pbk). First published as "Le Matin des Magiciens." Editions Gallimard, © 1960. (Book part, p. 188, 216, 232-234, 253. II). Note: some of these excerpts regarding Gurdjieff are reproduced in E. A. Tiryakian's "On the Margin of the Visible." Entry 432.

Perry, Robert L.

343. *The Shared Vision of Waldo Frank and Hart Crane*. Lincoln, Neb.: Univ. of Nebraska Studies: New Series # 33, May 1966. 73 p. notes, bib. (Pamphlet. III)

Perry, Whitall N.

344. *Gurdjieff*: In the Light of Tradition. Bedfont, Middlesex: Perennial Books, © 1978. 104 p., index. ISBN 0-900588-14-4, (pbk). (Book. I). First published as a series of essays in "Studies in Comparative Religion."
Part 1. "The Background." Vol. 8 # 4. Autumn 1974, p. 211-239.
Part 2. "The Teaching" Vol. 9 # 1. Winter 1975, p. 20-35.
Part 3. "The Phenomenon" Vol. 9 # 2. Spring 1975, p. 97-126.

Peters, Fritz (Arthur Anderson Peters. 1913-)

345. *Balanced Man: A Look at Gurdjieff Fifty Years Later.* 1978.

112 p. ISBN 0-70450-364-6

346. *Boyhood With Gurdjieff*. New York: Dutton, © 1964. 174 p. (Book. I)

347. *Gurdjieff*. Wildwood House, 1976. 330 p., ill., ISBN 7045-0219-4. (Contains Gurdjieff Remembered and Boyhood With Gurdjieff.)

348. *Gurdjieff Remembered*. London: Gollancz, © 1965. also, New York: Weiser, 1971. 159 p. ISBN 0-87728-142-4. (pbk). (Book. I)

Phillpotts, Dorothy

349. *Gurdjieff*: A New Path For the World? The Occult Observer. # 4, 1950. p. 253-260. 2200 wds. (Periodical Article. I)

Pogson, Beryl

350. *In the East My Pleasure Lies*: Studies in Shakespeare # 24. Folcroft, 1950. also, Haskell, 1974. ISBN 0-8383-1760-X.

351. *Maurice Nicoll*: A Portrait. London: Vincent Stuart, © 1961. 228 p., plates, index. (Book. I)

352. *The Work Life*. 1975. 142 p., index. (Book. I)

353. *Work Talks in Brighton*: 1936-1966. no date. 92 p. (Book. I)

Popenoe, Cris

354. *Books for Inner Development*: The Yes!. Guide. Wash. D.C.: Yes Bookshop, © 1976. 383 p., index. (Annotated bibliography on Gurdjieff, p. 154-158, lists 62 items. II)

Popoff, Irmis B.

355. *The Enneagrama of the Man of Unity*. New York: Weiser, 1978. 96 p. ISBN 0-87728-399-0, (pbk). (Book. II)

356. *Gurdjieff*: His Work, On Myself . . . With others . . . For the Work. 1st Edition. New York: Vantage, © 1969. 193 p., bib. also, New York: Weiser, 1978. ISBN 0-87728-417-2, (pbk). (Book. I)

Powys, Llewelyn

357. *The Verdict of Bridlegoose*. New York: Harcourt Brace, 1926. (Book part, p. 162-163. III)

Priestley, Jack B.

358.. *Man and Time*. London: Aldus Books, © 1964. also, New York: Dell, 1968. 365 p., ill., index. (Book part, Chapter 11. "Esoteric School" p. 295-314. (pbk.ed.). II)

359. Re. *J.B. Priestley*

See also: Cooper, S. "J. B. Priestley: Portrait of An Author." Entry 92.

360. *A Provisional Skeleton Index to* G. I. *Gurdjieff's "All and Everything."* Coombe Springs, Kingston-on-Thames, Surrey. The Institute for the Comparative Study of History, Philosophy and the Sciences, 1956. 65 p. (Unbound Mimeographed Typescript. I)

R.

Raine, Kathleen

361. *Golden Thigh or Feet of Clay?* [Review of G. I. Gurdjieff's "All and Everything." and P. D. Ouspensky's "In Search of the Miraculous."] The New Statesman and Nation. June 10, 1950. p. 664. 900 wds. (Book Review. I)

Rajneesh, Bhagwan Shree

362. *The Mustard Seed*: Discourses on the Sayings of Jesus taken from the Gospel According to Thomas./Compilation: Swami Amrit Pathik, Editor: Swami Satya Deva. Poona, India: Rajneesh Foundation, © 1975. 508 p. (Book parts, p. 41-44, 55-56, 59-60, 72-74. II)

Redman, Ben Ray

363. *Beelzebub from Mars.* [Review of G. I. Gurdjieff's "All and Everything."] The Saturday Review. June 24, 1950. p. 20. 850 wds. (Book Review. I)

Rees, Richard

364. *For Love or Money*: Studies in Personality and Essence. London: Secker & Warburg, © 1960. 191p. index, appendices. Book part, "Monsieur Gurdjieff or Essence and Personality," p. 131-145. also published as "Monsieur Gurdjieff," in The Twentieth Century. Nov., 1958. p. 432-443. 4500 wds. (Critical Essay. I)

Regamey, P.R.

365. *Monsieur Gurdjieff.* [Review of L. Pauwels' "Gurdjieff."]. La Vie Spirituelle. (Paris) Tome 92 #406, 1955. p. 515-518. (Book Review. II)

366. *Remembering Pytor Demianovich Ouspensky*: [A brochure celebrating the gift to Yale University Library of his papers & manuscripts]. New Haven: Yale Univ. Library, © 1978. 45 p. ill. (Brochure. II)

Rendall, V.

367. [*Letter to the Editor regarding "The Forest Philosophers"*, entry 151.] The New Statesman. Vol. 20 #519. Mar. 24, 1923. p. 719. (Letter. I)

368. [*Review of Bennett J. G. "Gurdjieff: Making A New World"*] Choice. Oct., 1974. p.1116. 200 wds. (Book Review. II)

369. [*Review of Collin R. "The Theory of Celestial Influence"*] Material for Thought. #7, 1977. p. 50-54. (Book Review. III)

370. [*Review of Gurdjieff G. I. "Meetings With Remarkable Men."*] The Christian Century. Vol. 80 #1. May 15, 1963. p. 648. 40 wds. (Book Review. I)

371. [*Review of Gurdjieff G. I. "Meetings With Remarkable Men."*] Punch. June 26, 1963. p. 939. 62 wds. (Book Review. I)

372. [*Review of Gurdjieff's Movements Demonstration* of Dec. 13, 1923. Paris]: Comoedia.
373. [*Review of Gurdjieff's Movements Demonstration* of Dec. 13, 1923. Paris]: Le Temps.
374. [*Review of "Gurdjieff: Views from the Real World."*] Booklist. Vol. 70 #1. Dec. 15, 1973. p. 406. 83 wds. (Book Review. I)
375. [*Review of "Gurdjieff: Views from the Real World."*] Books and Bookman. Vol. 19. April [1974]. p. 107-108. (Book Review. I)
376. [*Review of "Gurdjieff: Views from the Real World."*] Choice. Vol. 11 #1. May 1974. p. 418. 160 wds. (Book Review. I)
377. [*Review of Travers P. L. "About the Sleeping Beauty".*] Material for Thought #7, 1977. p. 57-59. (Book Review. III)

Reymond, Lizelle

378. *The Samkhya of India*: A Conscious Struggle Toward Reality. in "Sacred Tradition and Present Need." Edited by Jacob Needleman. p. 59-74. Entry 295. (Essay in Collection. III)
379. *To Live Within.* /Translated by Nancy Pearson & Stanley Spiegelberg with a forward by Jacob Needleman. New York: Doubleday, © 1971. also, Baltimore: Penguin, 1973. 271 p. First Published as *La Vie dans la Vie*. Editions du Mont-Blanc, © 1969. (Book parts, p. 74, 129-137, 162-164, 167, 170, 171, 180, 187-188, 204-205, 213, also consider 141. II)

Reyner, John H.

380. *The Diary of a Modern Alchemist.* London: Spearman, © 1974. 154 p., index. SBN 85435-172-8. (Book. II)
381. *God Beyond Time.*
382. *A Philosophy of Delight.* London: Watkins, ©1976. 66 p. (Book. II)
383. *Universe of Relationships.*

Roberts, Carl Eric Bechhofer

384. *The Forest Philosophers*. (by C. E. Bechhofer). The Century Illustrated Monthly Magazine. Vol. 86. May 1924. p. 66-78. 7000 wds. Also published (by C. E. Bechhofer Roberts) in World Today (London). Vol. 44. June 1924. p. 9-16. 5000 wds. [Edited Version] Photo of Gurdjieff. (Periodical Essay. I)
385. *In Deniken's Russia*. (Arno Reprint)

Rosenbaum, Ron

386. *Playboy Interview*: Bob Dylan, a candid conversation with the visionary whose songs changed the times. Playboy Magazine. Vol. 25 # 3. March 1978. p. 61-90. 12,000 wds. (Periodical Interview. Ref. to Gurdjieff, p. 78-81, 88. III)

Rosenfeld, Edward

387. *The Book of Highs*. New York: Quadrangle, © 1973. 251 p., bib., index. (Book part, p. 161-162. III)

Rosenshine, Annette

388. *Life's Not A Paragraph*. Unpublished manuscript, © 1964.

267 p. The Bancroft Library, Univ. of Calif. at Berkeley. Microfilm # F68/154. (Microfilmed typescript, part, p. 185-198, 212-214. II)

Roszak, Theodore

389. *Unfinished Animal*: The Aquarian Frontier and the Evolution of Consciousness. New York: Harper & Row, © 1975. Harper Colophon Books, 1977. 271 p. ISBN 0-06-090537-9 (pbk), index. (Book parts. I)

Rowley, Peter

390. *New Gods in America*: An Informal Investigation into the New Religions of American Youth Today. New York: McKay, 1971. (Book part, p. 14-24. II)

Rule, Jane

391. *Lesbian Images*. New York: Doubleday, © 1975. also, Markham, Ontario: Simon & Schuster, 1976. (Pocket Book Edition). 257 p., notes, bib., index. (Book part re. Margaret Anderson, p. 152-161. III)

392. [*Rumi*]: *The Whirling Ecstasy*. [A selection from "The Lives of the Gnostics" by Aflaki, written between 1318 and 1335 and translated into French by C. Huart in "Les Saints des Derviches Tourneurs," Paris, 1918-1922.] Mexico City: Ediciones Sol, 1954. 28 p., ill. (Pamphlet. III)

S.

Saurat, Denis

393. *A Visit to Gourdyev*. The Living Age. Jan., 1934. p. 427-433. 3500 wds. (Periodical Article. I)

Savage, R. S.

394. *The New Gnosticism*. [Review of G. I. Gurdjieff's "All and Everything."] The Spectator. Vol. 184. April 28, 1950. p. 587-588. 650 wds. (Book review. I)

Schorer, Mark

395. *Sinclair Lewis*: An American Life. New York: McGraw Hill, 1961. (Book part, p. 377-378. III)

Schumacher, E. F.

396. *A Guide for the Perplexed*. New York: Harper & Row, © 1977. (Perennial Library), 1979. ISBN 0-06-080463-7 (pbk). 147 p., notes. (Book. II)

Seabrook, William

397. *Witchcraft*: Its Power in the World Today. New York: Harcourt Brace, 1940. also, New York: Lancer Books, (pbk). (Book part, p. 204-216. II)

398. *Search*: [Journey on the Inner Path] / Edited by Jean

Sulzberger with an introduction by Henri Traco]. New York: Harper & Row, © 1979. 151 p., ill. ISBN 0-06-067766-X (cloth) 0-06-067765-1 (pbk). Contains entry 449, P. L. Travers' essay on Peter Brooks' film of "Meetings With Remarkable Men." (Book, collection of essays and excerpts. II)

Seaver, Edwin

399. *As of a Saturday Afternoon*. A Journal of Our Time. Number 2, 1979; p. 25-26. (Periodical Article. I)

400. *Solving the Human Enigma*. [Review of G. I. Gurdjieff's "Meetings With Remarkable Men."] Saturday Review. May 18, 1963. p. 27-28. 850 wds. photo of Gurdjieff. (Book Review. I)

401. *Secret Talks With* Mr. G.: To A Specially Formed Group As Recollected by His Pupils. [Authorship uncertain, has been attributed to E. J. Gold.] [Nevada City, Calif.]: IDHHB, © 1978. 163 p. photos [apparently of Gurdjieff, but whose authenticity has been questioned.] index. ISBN 0-89556-001-1. (Book. I)

402. *Secret Talks* [With G.]: Vol. II. [Authorship uncertain, has been attributed to E. J. Gold.] [Nevada City, CA]: IDHHB, © 1979. Private publication, consists of 24 chapters to be released bi-weekly on a subscription basis as of May, 1979. (Unbound Mimeographed Typescript I)

Selver, Paul

403. *Orage and the New Age Circle*: Reminiscences and Reflections. London: Allen & Unwin, © 1959. 100 p., index. (Book part, p. 73-78. III)

Shah, Idries

404. *The Exploits of the Incomparable Mulla Nasrudin*. London: Jonathan Cape, © 1966. 158 p. ISBN 0-224-60214-4. (Book. III)

405. *The Pleasantries of the Incredible Mulla Nasrudin*. New York: Dutton, © 1968. 218 p. SBN 0-525-47306-8, (pbk). (Book. III)

406. *Special Problems in the Study of Sufi Ideas*. Turnbridge Wells: Society for the Understanding of the Foundation of Ideas, 1966. (Pamphlet. III)

407. Re. *Idries Shah*
See also: Lefort, Rafael, reputed pseudonym of Idries Shah.

Sheckley, Robert

408. *Untouched by Human Hands*. New York: Ballantine, 1954. 169 p. (Book. Fiction - Short Story Collection, part. Story titled "Warm", p. 97-107. II)

Simon, Linda

409. *The Biography of Alice B. Toklas*. New York: Doubleday, 1977. plates, notes, bib., index. (Book part, p. 87, 137-139, 206, 311. III)

Smith, Adam
410. *Powers of Mind*. New York: Random, © 1975. also, New York: Ballantine, 1976. (pbk) 419 p., notes, bib., ISBN 0-345-25426-0-195. (Book parts, p. 239-248 re. G. I. Gurdjieff, p. 252-267 re. Oscar Ichazo, p. 293-313 re. John Lilly. II)
Smith, Eleanor T.
411. [*Review of K. Hulme's "Undiscovered Country*"] Library Journal. Vol. 91 # 4. Nov. 15, 1966. p. 5600. 200 wds. (Book Review. II)
Speeth, Kathleen Riordan
412. *The Gurdjieff Work*. Berkeley: And/Or Press, © 1976. 114 p. ill., notes. ISBN 0-915904-19-5 (pbk). also, New York: Pocket Books, 1978. 176 p. ISBN 0-671-81841-4 (pbk). Earlier version published as an essay in "Transpersonal Psychologies," entry 426. (Book. I)
413. Re. Kathleen R. Speeth
See also: Interview with Kathleen Speeth et al, on New Dimensions Tape Set # 1133, "Gurdjieff," entry 299.
414. *Spiritual Community Guide # 4, 1979*. San Rafael, Calif.: Spiritual Community Publications, © 1978. 256 p. (Directory parts re. Gurdjieff Groups, p. 46, 95, 107, 127-128, 134, 143, 154, 159, 230, 238, 247, 248. Addresses. II)
Sprigge, Elizabeth
415. *Gertrude Stein*: Her Life and Work. London: Hamish Hamilton, 1957. 277 p., plates, bib., index. (Book part, p. 159-161. III)
Stavely, L.
416. *Memories of Gurdjieff*. Aurora Or.: Two Rivers Press, © 1978. 74 p. ISBN 0-89756-000-0 (cloth). (Book. I)
Note: Two Rivers Press. Box 626 Aurora, Or. 97002.
Stein, Leo
417. *Journey Into the Self*: being the letters, papers & journals of Leo Stein./ Edited by Edmund Fuller. New York: Crown, © 1950. 330 p., index. (Book part, p. 158. III)
418. *Sufi Times*: A Fourth Way Publication. Crestline, Calif.,: IDHHB bimonthly. Vol. 1 to 6, 1977-1978. Edited by Cybele and E. J. Gold. ISSN 0149-5135. Superseded by *Wings*, Sept., 1978, entry 493. (Periodical. III)
Sugrue, Thomas
419. *Pursuit of Esoteric Lore*. [Review of P. D. Ouspensky's "In Search of the Miraculous."] New York Herald Tribune Book Review. Dec. 11, 1949. p. 16. 1100 wds. (Book Review. I)
Sussman, Aaron
420. *In Search of Hidden Mysteries*. [Review of G. I. Gurdjieff's "Meetings With Remarkable Men."] Herald Tribune: Books. Aug. 18, 1963. p. 6. 1000 wds. (Book Review. I)

Swayne, Martin (Pseudonym of Maurice Nicoll)

421. *The Blue Germ*. London: Hodder & Stoughton. 1918. 279 p. (Book, Fiction. III)

Sykes, Gerald

422. *Philosophical Meanderings*. [Review of G.I. Gurdjieff's "All and Everything."] New York Times Book Review Section. Mar. 19, 1950. p. 50. 280 wds. (Book Review. I)

T.

Tart, Charles

423. *Science, States of Consciousness and Spiritual Experience*: The Need for State-Specific Sciences. in "Transpersonal Psychologies" p. 9-58, edited by Charles Tart, entry 426, (Essay in Collection. II)

424. *Some Assumptions of Orthodox Western Psychology*. in "Transpersonal Psychologies" p. 59-111, edited by Charles Tart, entry 426. (Essay in Collection. II)

425. *States of Human Consciousness*. New York: Dutton, 1975. 305 p., bib., index. (Book part, p. 136, 164-168, 238, 282. III)

426. *Transpersonal Psychologies*. /Edited with an introduction and three essays by Charles Tart. New York: Harper and Row, © 1975. 485 p. (cloth). also, Harper Colophon, 1977. 504 p., ref., bib., indices. (Book. II) Contains eleven essays including—

    Lilly, John. C. & Hart, J. E. "The Arica Training," Entry 257.

    Speeth, K. R. "Gurdjieff," entry 412.

427. Re. *Charles Tart*

    See also: Matson, K. "Psychology Today Omnibook," p. 461-465, entry 271.

    New Dimensions Foundation, Tape Set #1133, "Gurdjieff"; Interview with Charles Tart et al. Entry 299.

Tedlock, Jr., E. W.

428. *D.H. Lawrence's Annotations of Ouspensky's "Tertium Organum."* Texas Studies in Literature and Language: A Journal of the Humanities. Vol. II #2. Summer 1960. p. 206-218. 5000 wds. (Periodical Essay. III)

Thatchuk, Danny (Dr. Bundolo)

429. *Cat and Mouse with E. J. Gold*: As Interviewed by Danny (Dr. Bundolo) Thatchuk on C.B.C. [Canadian Broadcasting Corp.] Radio. New Directions: A Lifestyle Magazine. [Aug. 1977] #27. p. 40-50. (Periodical Interview. III)

430. *Thomas De Hartmann*. Musical Courier. May 1956. p. 26. 140

wds. (Obituary. III)

431. *Thomas De Hartmann (1886-1956).* [New York: Boosey & Hawkes], no date. 10 unnumbered pages. Contains a biographical sketch, some critiques, a list of musical compositions and a photo. (Pamphlet. III)

Tiryakian, Edward A.

432. *On the Margin of the Visible*: Sociology, the Esoteric and the Occult./Edited by E. A. Tiryakian. New York: Wiley & Sons, 1974. Contains excerpts on p. 55-58 & 169-176, from Louis Pauwels' "Morning of the Magicians," entry 341, regarding Gurdjieff. (Book part. III)

Toklas, Alice B.

433. *Staying On Alone*: Letters of Alice B. Toklas./Edited by Edward Burns. New York: Liveright, 1973. 426 p., ill., index. (Book. III)

Toomer, Jean (Nathan Eugene Toomer. 1894-1967)

434. *Chapters from "Earth Being" An Unpublished Autobiography.* The Black Scholar. Jan. 1971. p. 3-14. (Excerpts from an Autobiography published as a Periodical Article. III)

435. *Essentials:* Definitions and Aphorisms. Chicago: Private Edition, © 1931. 64 unnumbered pages. (Booklet. II)

436. *Living is Developing.* Doylestown, Penn.: Mill House Pamphlets, 1937. (Psychological Series #1). (Pamphlet. II)

437. *Mr. Costyve Duditch.* The Dial. Vol. LXXXV #6. Dec. 1928. p. 460-476. 7000 wds. (Periodical, Short Story. II)

438. *A New Force for Co-operation.* [Formerly titled "The Spiritualization of America."] Adelphi. Vol. 9 #1. Oct., 1934. p. 25-31. 2600 wds. (Periodical Article. III)

439. *Reflections.* [Four Aphorisms] The Dial. Vol. LXXXVI #4. April, 1929. p. 314. (Periodical Filler. II)

440. *Work Ideas I.* Doylestown, Penn.: Mill House Pamphlets, 1937. (Psychological Series #2). (Pamphlet. I)

441. *York Beach.* in The New American Caravan: A Yearbook of American Literature./Edited by Alfred Kreymborg et al. New York: Macaulay, © 1929. P.12-83. (Fiction. III)

442. Re. *Jean Toomer*

See also: Bone, R. "Down Home." Entry 64.
Dillard, M. "Jean Toomer." Entry 127.
Fulinwider, S. P. "Jean Toomer." Entry 161.
Hughs, L. "The Big Sea." Entry 213.
Munson, G. "The Significance of Jean Toomer." Entry 287.
Turner, D. T. "In A Minor Chord." Entry 452.

Note: Most of Jean Toomer's writings remain unpublished. For descriptions of some of this material and how extensively it was influenced by Gurdjieff; see Bone, entry 64 and

Turner, entry 452. The full body of Toomer's manuscripts are housed in the Fisk University Library, 17th Ave. North, Nashville, Tenn.

443. *Town Hall*: Music By Thomas de Hartmann. Musical Courier. June 1956. p. 39. 260 wds. (Musical Performance Review. III)

Tracol, Henri

444. *George Ivanovitch Gurdjieff*: Man's Awakening and the Practice of Remembering Oneself. Bray: Guild Press, 1968. Reprinted 1977. 19 p. (Pamphlet. I)

445. *Thus Spake Beelzebub.* Maitreya #6, 1977. p. 13-20. (© by Triangle Editions, New York). 4000 wds. (Periodical Essay. I)

446. Re. *Henri Tracol*

See also: "Search"/Edited by Jean Sulzberger with an introduction by Henri Tracol. Entry 398.

Travers, P(amela) L(yndon) (1906-)

447. *About the Sleeping Beauty*./Illustrated by Charles Keeping. New York: McGraw-Hill, © 1975. 111 p. ISBN 0-07-065123-X (cloth). (Book, Children's Stories, Folklore. II)

448. *George Ivanovitch Gurdjieff*. [Toronto]: Traditional Studies Press, 1973. 8 p., photo of Gurdjieff, 2600 wds. ISBN 0-919608-08-6. (Pamphlet. I) This is an amplified version of an article titled "Gurdjieff" that appeared in "Man, Myth and Magic." p. 1188-1189, 2400 wds., entry 267. (Encyclopedia Article. I)

449. *Meetings With Remarkable Men*: One Man's Search Becomes a Film. in "Search"/Edited by Jean Sulzberger, p. 101-109, entry (Essay in Collection. I)

450. *Myth, Symbol and Tradition.* in Sacred Tradition and Present Need./Edited by Jacob Needleman, p. 111-124. Entry 295. (Essay in Collection. II)

451. Re. *P. L. Travers*

See also: Commire, A. "Something About the Author." Vol. 4. p. 208-209. Entry 91.
Kunitz, S. J. "Twentieth Century Authors" and "First Supplement." Entries 241 & 242.
Travers, P. L. "Mary Poppins," Series of children's stories published by Harcourt Brace.

Turner, Darwin T.

452. *In A Minor Chord*: Three Afro-American Writers and Their Search. Carbondale & Edwardsville: Southern Illinois Univ. Press, 1971. 153 p., notes, bib., index. (Book part re. Jean Toomer, p. 1-59. II)

Twombly, Robert C.

453. *Frank Lloyd Wright*: An Interpretive Biography. New York: Harper & Row, 1973. (Book III)

454. *Organic Living*: Frank Lloyd Wright's Taliesin Fellowship and

Georgi Gurdjieff's Institute for the Harmonious Development of Man. Wisconsin Magazine of History. Winter 1974-1975. p. 126-135. photos, one of Gurdjieff. (Periodical Essay. I)

U.

Unterecker, John

455. *Voyager*: A Life of Hart Crane. New York: Farrar, Straus & Giroux, © 1969. 787 p., index. (Book part, p. 358, 500-504. III)

V.

Vassi, Marco

456. *The Metasex Manifesto*: erotic tales of the absurdly real. New York: Bantam, 1976. 212 p. ISBN 0-553-02441-8. Originally published as "Metasex, Mirth & Madness" by Penthouse Press, 1975. (Book parts, p. 110, 201. III)
457. *The Stoned Apocalypse*. New York: Pocket Books, 1973. 224 p. SBN 671-78286-X. First published by Trident, 1972. (Book part, p. 1-24. II)

Vaysse, Jean

458. *Toward Awakening*: An approach to the teaching left by Gurdjieff. San Francisco: Far West Undertakings, © 1978. 170 p. ISBN 0-914480-04-9 (cloth). (Book. I)
Note: Far West Undertakings. 3231 Pierce St., San Francisco, CA 94123.

Von Harten, Marjorie

459. *A Way of Living*. Sherborne: Coombe Springs Press, © 1974. 83 p. ISBN 0-900306-08-4. (Book. I)

W.

Walker, Kenneth (Macfarlane) (1882-1966)

460. *The Circle of Life*. London: Cape, 1944.
461. *Commentary on Age*. London: Cape, 1952. 192 p. index. (Book. II)
462. *Diagnosis of Man*. London: Cape, 1942. also, Harmondsworth: Penguin, 1962. (Revised Edition) 259 p., bib. (pbk). (Book. II)
463. *George Gurdjieff*: A Memoir. World Review (London). Feb., 1950. p. 35-37, 78. photo of Gurdjieff. 2000 wds. (Periodical Article. I)

464. *The Greatness of Gurdjieff*. The Saturday Book—10th Year/ Edited by Leonard Russell. London: Hutchinson, 1950. p. 86-91. photo of Gurdjieff. 1800 wds. (Yearbook Article. I)
465. *The Log of the Ark.* /by Kenneth Walker and Geoffrey Boumphrey. London: Constable, 1923. also, London: Cape, 1958. 214 p., ill. (Book, Children's Fiction. III)
466. *The Making of Man.* London: Routledge & Kegan, © 1963. 163 p. bib., index, plates. (Book. I)
467. *A Study of Gurdjieff's Teaching.* London: Cape, 1957. (cloth). also, London: Cape, 1965. (pbk). also, New York: Award Books & London: Tandem Books, 1969. 221 p., index. (pbk). also, New York: Weiser, 1974. ISBN 0-87728-262-5 (pbk). (Book. I)
468. *Venture With Ideas.* London: Cape, © 1951. also, New York: Pellegrini & Cadahy, 1952. also, New York: Weiser, 1972. 192 p. ISBN 0-87728-209-9, (pbk). (Book. I)

Watkins, Mary M.

469. *Waking Dreams*. New York: Harper & Row, © 1976. 174 p., bib., index. (Book part, p. 16. III)

Watts, Alan

470. *In My Own Way*: An Autobiography 1915-1965. New York: Pantheon, ©1972. (cloth). also, New York: Random, 1973 (Vintage Books). 466 p., index. ISBN 0-394-71951-4, (pbk). (Book parts. III)

Webb, James

471. *Georgi Ivanovitch Gurdjieff.* in Encyclopedia of the Unexplained./Edited by Richard Cavindish, entry 78. p. 107-109. 2000 wds. photo of Gurdjieff. (Encyclopedia Article. I)
472. *The Harmonious Circle.* New York: Putnam, and London: Thames & Hudson. Forthcoming since 1974. (Book. I)
473. *Letter to the editor*: re. L. P. Elwell-Sutton's "Sufism & Pseudo-Sufism." See entry 139.
474. *The Occult Establishment.* La Salle, Ill.: Opencourt, 1976. (A Library Press Book) 535 p., index. (Book parts. II)

Weber, Brom

475. *Hart Crane*: A Biographical and Critical Study. New York: Bodley Press, © 1948. 452 p., bib., index. (Book part, p. 213-215. III)

Welch, Louise

476. *The Old Man Rides A Bicycle*. Toronto: Traditional Studies Press, © 1972. 30 unnumbered pages. ISBN 0-919608-06-X (cloth) 0-919608-07-8 (pbk). (Book, Children's Fiction. I)
477. *The Quest in Our Time.* A Journal of Our Time. Number 1, 1977. Entry 196. p. 5-11. 2000 wds. (Periodical Article. II)
478. *Wisdom Builds Her House.* A Journal of Our Time. Number 2, 1979; p. 35-38. (Periodical Essay. II)

Welch, W. J.

479. *What Happened In Between*: A Doctor's Story. New York: Braziller, © 1972. 208 p. SBN 8076-0660-X. (Book. II)

White, Nelia Gardner

480. *Daughter of Time*: The Life of Katherine Mansfield in novel form. London: Constable, 1942. 244 p. (Book. III)

Wilbur, Ken

481. *The Spectrum of Consciousness*. Wheaton, Ill.: Theosophical Pub. House, 1977. (A Quest Book) 374 p., bib., index. (Book parts, p. 19, 181-182. III)

Williams, Sheldon

482. *Gurdjieff Through Many Eyes*. [Review of L. Pauwels' "Gurdjieff"] Contemporary Review. June 1964. p. 316-321. 2200 wds. (Book Review. II)

Wilson, Collin

483. *Human Factory*. [Review of "Gurdjieff: Views from the Real World."] The Spectator. Mar. 2, 1974. p. 269-270. 1100 wds. (Book Review. I)

484. *Men of Mystery*. /Edited with an introduction by Collin Wilson. London: Allen, 1977. 206 p. ISBN 0-352-39593-1 (pbk). (Book part, p. 38-52, "Gurdjieff" by Collin Wilson. This collection has been adapted as a television series, see entry 198 Essay in Collection. I)

485. *The Mind Parasites*. Oakland Calif.: Oneric Press, 1972. 222 p. (Book, Fiction. III)

486. *Mysteries*: [An Investigation into the occult, the paranormal & the supernatural]. New York: Putnams, © 1978. 667 p., index, bib. (Book. III)

487. *The Occult*: A History. New York: Random, © 1971. 603 p., bib., index. (Book part, p. 387-414. II)

488. *The Outsider*. Boston: Houghton Mifflin, 1956. index. (Book parts. III)

489. *Religion and the Rebel*. London: Gollancz, 1957. 333 p., notes, index. (Book parts. III)

490. *The Strength to Dream*. London: Gollancz, 1963. (cloth). also, London: Abacus, 1976. (pbk) 254 p., index. (Book parts. III)

Wilson, P.W.

491. *Close Up Portraits of Our Modern Prophets and Mystics*. [Review of R. Landau's "God Is My Adventure."] New York Times Book Review. May 3, 1936. p. 9. 1500 wds. photo. (Book Review. III)

Wilson, Robert Anton

492. *Cosmic Trigger*: Final Secret of the Illuminati./Illustrated by John Thompson. Berkeley: And/Or Press, © 1977. 269 p., notes, index. ISBN 0-915904-29-2 (pbk). (Book parts. III)

493. *Wings*. /Edited by Cybele & E. J. Gold. Nevada City, Calif:

IDHHB. bimonthly. Vol. 1 #1, Sept.-Oct., 1978. ISSN 0161-6331. Supersedes "Sufi Times," entry 418 (Periodical. III)

494. *Wisdom Through Mystification*. [Review of L. Pauwels' "Gurdjieff," F. Peters' "Boyhood With Gurdjieff" and K. Walker's "Making of Man."] The Times (London) Literary Supplement. Thurs. Mar. 12, 1964. p. 213. 2500 wds. (Book Review. II)

495. *Wise Man from the East*. [Review of K. Walker's "Venture With Ideas."] Time (Magazine). Vol. 59. Jan. 28, 1952. p. 100-102. photo of Gurdjieff. 1000 wds. (Book Review. II)

Wolfe, Edwin

496. *Episodes With Gurdjieff*. [Millerton, N.Y.]: Far West Press, © 1974. 38 p. (Book. I)

Wolfe, Geoffry

497. *Great Lady*. [Review of Margaret Anderson's "The Fiery Fountains," "My Thirty Years' War" and "The Strange Necessity."] Newsweek. May 25, 1970. p. 112-114. 750 wds. photo. (Book Review. III)

Wright, Frank Lloyd

498. *An Autobiography*. London: Faber, 1946. 486 p. (Book part, p. 442. III)

499. *At Taliesin*. The Capitol (Madison, Wisconsin) Times. Aug. 26, 1934. (Newspaper Article re. Gurdjieff. I)

Wright, (Olgivana) Mrs. Frank Lloyd

500. *The Last Days of Katherine Mansfield*. The Bookman. Vol. 73. Mar., 1931. p. 6-13. (Periodical Article. II)

501. *Our House*. New York: Horizon Press, 1959. 308 p. (Book parts, p. 210, 275. III)

502. *The Struggle Within*. New York: Horizon Press, © 1955. 176 p. ISBN 0-8180-1311-7 (cloth). (Book. I)

503. Re. *Frank Lloyd and Olgivana Wright*

See also: Twombly, R. C. "Frank L. Wright," entry 453.
Twombly, R. C. "Organic Living," entry 454.

Y.

Young, James Carruthers

504. *An Experiment At Fontainebleau*: A Personal Reminiscence. The New Adelphi. Vol. 1 #1. Sept. 1927. p. 26-40. (Periodical Essay. I)

Z.

Zigrosser, Carl

505. *Gurdjieff*. The New Republic. June 5, 1929. p. 66-69. 3400

wds. (Periodical Article. I)

Zodec, G.

506. *Lessons in Religion for a Skeptical World*. Mexico City: Ediciones Sol. 1956. 37 p. (Pamphlet. III)

507. *Zona Gale is Dead*: Wisconsin Writer. New York Times. Wed. Dec. 28, 1938. p. 21. photo. 1700 wds. (Obituary. III)

Zuber, Rene

508. *Qui etes-vous Monsieur Gurdjieff?* Paris: Courrier du Livre, 1977. An excerpt translated into English by Jane McWhinney et al is published as *First Impressions of Gurdjieff* in A Journal of Our Time. Number 2, 1979, p. 73-79. (Book. I)

Never travel in search of knowledge unless you are sent. The desire to travel for learning is a test, not a command.

Bahaudin Naqshibandi in
Shah, I., *Thinkers of the East*.